A FABER CRITICAL GUIDE
Brian Friel

_____ ** sta Jones** was formerly Reader in Theatre Arts and
of Drama at Goldsmiths College, University of
on. She has published on J. M. Synge, Sean O'Casey,
vid Mamet, the history and techniques of English act-
and performance processes; directed plays of the
ish classical and modern European theatre at venues
tain, Ireland, mainland Europe (East and West), and
America; and created programmes for London
nd Television and the British Council. She is
ntly project co-ordinator for CONCEPTS (Con-
m for the Co-ordination of European Performance
heatre Studies) and Artistic Director of NXT (New
Theatre).

aismith, the series editor of the Faber Critical
s, was a Lecturer in Drama at the University of
n, Goldsmiths' College, for twenty-five years and
ectures in Drama for the Central University of Iowa
ndon. His other published work includes Student
es to 'Top Girls' by Caryl Churchill (Methuen,
t), 'The Rover' by Aphra Behn (Methuen, 1993),
oss Oka' by Robert Holman (Methuen, 1994) and
Country's Good' by Timberlake Wertenbaker
huen, 1995).

A FABER CRITICAL GUIDE
Brian Friel

Philadelphia, Here I Come!
Translations
Making History
Dancing at Lughnasa

NESTA JONES

faber and faber
LONDON·NEW YORK

for Dominic, Jackie and Isobel

First published in 2000
by Faber and Faber Limited
3 Queen Square London WC1N 3AU
Published in the United States by Faber and Faber Inc.
an affiliate of Farrar, Straus and Giroux, New York

Photoset by Wilmaset Ltd, Birkenhead, Wirral
Printed in England by Mackays of Chatham plc, Chatham, Kent

A CIP record for this book
is available from the British Library
ISBN 0-571-19779-5

2 4 6 8 10 9 7 5 3 1

Contents

Editor's Preface

The *Faber Critical Guides* provide comprehensive introductions to major dramatists of the twentieth century.

The need to make an imaginative leap when reading dramatic texts is well known. Plays are written with live performance in mind. Often a theatre audience is confronted with a stage picture, a silent character or a vital movement – any of which might be missed in a simple 'reading'. The *Guides* advise you what to look for.

All plays emerge from a context – a background – the significance of which may vary but needs to be appreciated if the original impact of the play is to be understood. A writer may be challenging convention, reacting to the social and political life of the time or engaging with intellectual ideas. The *Guides* provide coverage of the appropriate context in each case.

A number of key texts are examined in each Guide in order to provide a sound introduction to the individual dramatists. Studying only one work is rarely enough to make informed judgements about the style and originality of writer's work. Considering several plays is also the only way to follow a writer's development.

Finally, the *Guides* are meant to be read in conjunction with the play texts. 'The play's the thing' and must always be the primary concern. Not only are all playwrights different but every play has its own distinctive features which the *Guides* are concerned to highlight.

Note on References

All page references to the plays by Brian Friel discussed in this book are to the re-set single editions of the plays published by Faber and Faber in 2000.

Full details of critical works and other material quoted in the book are given in the Select Bibliography.

ACKNOWLEDGEMENTS

I should like to thank the following for their help in the preparation of this volume: Mairead Delaney, Archivist, National Theatre of Ireland; Nicola Scadding, Archivist, Royal National Theatre of Great Britain; Dr Brian Singleton, School of Drama, Samuel Beckett Centre, Trinity College, Dublin; Steven Dykes; Carol King; Eileen and Neil Macfarlane; Caroline McCloskey; and Simon Trussler of Country Setting for creating the map on page 4.

N.J.

Introduction

Friel the Ulsterman

Brian Friel was born in Killyclogher, close to the town of Omagh in County Tyrone, in January 1929. He claims: 'I have two birth certificates, one which says my birthday falls on January 9th, another which favours January 10th' ('Meet Brian Friel', *Irish Press*, 29 April 1962, p. 10). Friel's charming response to this ambiguity is the observation 'Perhaps I'm twins,' but a sense of duality, of personal division and estrangement, was to become a theme he explored later in his writing, most explicitly in *Philadelphia, Here I Come!* He goes on to tell us that, although he is known as Brian, 'I was baptised Bernard Patrick.' The substitution by his parents of Bernard for the obviously preferred Brian is perhaps a telling gesture. Friel was born into a recently partitioned country that was further divided in Northern Ireland along sectarian lines. The Friels were a Catholic family living in a predominantly Protestant constituency and maybe to avoid any difficulty with the authorities of registering a Gaelic name, an Anglicised version was adopted. The ritual of naming and the importance of names as a key to individual and national identity, and the problem of communication between cultures are major issues that Friel later addressed in his masterpiece *Translations*.

Friel is an Ulsterman – his father, Patrick Friel, came from Derry and his mother from Glenties in County

Donegal. Both sets of grandparents were Irish-speaking, as was his mother. Friel and his father learnt Irish at school. Patrick Friel was a schoolmaster, Principal of the National Primary School at Culmore, which Friel attended. He has two sisters, who also became teachers, and there was a younger brother who died in infancy. His mother was a civil servant. In 1939, when Friel was ten, the family moved to Derry, where his father took up a new teaching post. Friel says of the city: 'There are two aspects to Derry: one was of a gentle and, in those days, sleepy town; the other was of a frustrating and frustrated town in which the majority of people were disinherited. From the first point of view it was an easygoing town in which to grow up, but from a spiritual point of view, it wasn't a good town' (Hickey and Smith, p. 221).

Friel was a member of the first generation of the Northern Irish Catholic minority to grow up under 'triumphalist Unionism'. Derry, however, was peculiar in that the Catholic constituency made up the bulk of the population. In the quotation, Friel highlights the problem of living in a community where the majority were denied basic civil rights by an ascendant Protestant minority which, through a variety of political machinations and manoeuvres, conspired to maintain control. Therefore, despite the fact that his family was middle class and economically comfortable, Friel shared with his fellow Catholics a sense of frustration and disinheritence. In contrast Friel spent his holidays a short distance across the border with his mother's family at Glenties in rural County Donegal. Here he experienced a freedom and a place to which his imagination could respond. The emotional significance of this locale pervades his work.

After completing his secondary education at St Columb's College in Derry, Friel went south in 1946 to St Patrick's College, the national seminary at Maynooth, County Kildare, to study for the Catholic priesthood. Friel is reticent about this period, which he describes as 'an awful experience, it nearly drove me cracked. It is one thing I want to forget. I never talk about it – the priesthood' (Fintan O'Toole, 'Neither priest nor politician, but observer and playwright', *Irish Times*, 23 April 1990, p. 8). He moved to St Joseph's College in Belfast to train to be a teacher. Of the career that followed in primary and secondary schools in Derry Friel says, 'I don't regret the teaching – in fact I liked the teaching.' However, Friel found that conditions in the city had not changed. He became a member of the Nationalist Party for a number of years but did not follow his father, who had served three terms as a Nationalist Party member of Derry Corporation, into local politics: 'I resigned ... because I felt the party had lost initiative.' Instead he was writing in his spare time. 'There was no background of writing in my family and I don't know how much of my talent is indigenous. I don't think there are any other writers in Derry. Some people feel that if you are a writer or painter you must live in a colony, but I find writing a very private and personal existence and I was aware of no sense of loss at being the only writer in Derry' (Hickey and Smith, pp. 221–2).

In 1954 he married Anne Morrison. By 1960 he had two radio plays, several short stories and regular contributions to prestigious journals, such as *The New Yorker*, to his credit. He gave up his teaching job, became a full-time writer and with his growing family (eventually five children) moved to Donegal. 'The sense of frustration

Inishowgn Peninsula
Burnfoot
Buncrana
Rathmullan
Raphoe
Gortahork
Strabane
Glenties
Killybegs
Ballyshannon
Bundoran

Belmullet

NORTH CHANNEL

Giant's Causeway

RATHLIN I.

Londonderry

Dungiven
Sperrin Mts

ANTRIM

Belfast

DONEGAL

ULSTER

Omagh
Dungannon

Tullyhogue

Donegal Bay

Blackwater

FERMANAGH

Enniskillen

DOWN

Armagh

Tandragee

Sligo

Newry

SLIGO

LEITRIM

MONAGHAN

MAYO

Roosky

CAVAN

Castlereagh

CONNAUGHT

L. Mask

Roscommon

LONGFORD

Dundalk

Mellifont
Loch Owel

Boyne R.

Lough
Corrib

L. Ree

MEATH

Oughterard

GALWAY

WEST MEATH
Athlone

Hill of
Tara

Galway

Maynooth

DUBLIN

Galway Bay

L.
Derg

LEINSTER

KILDARE

WICKLOW
Wicklow

CLARE

Ennis

Shannon

TIPPERARY

CARLOW

Limerick

Kilkenny
KILKENNY

R. Shannon

LIMERICK

WEXFORD

MUNSTER

Waterford
WATERFORD

Killarney

Blackwater R.

KERRY

CORK

Dungarven

Cork

Bandon

Bantry

Kinsale

Skibbereen

IRISH SEA

which I felt under the tight and immovable Unionist regime became distasteful. One was always conscious of discrimination in Derry. Still, I don't think the gap is too wide to be breached. People are pliable and generous. In a family the most outrageous things may be said, yet within a week, although they have not been forgotten, they can be glossed over. The same can apply to our political and religious differences' (Hickey and Smith, p. 221).

It is important to remember that in the three decades that Friel lived in Northern Ireland, two of them in the city of Derry, political tensions remained high, sustained by a major IRA campaign during the 1950s and other incidents of sectarian violence. In the years to come terrorist offensives, on both sides of the sectarian divide, and outbreaks of civil disorder in response to the continuing British military presence in the Province, were to escalate. Friel's analogy of the family is interesting. The nation as family had long been distressed by tribal conflict of one kind or another and the legacy of colonisation caused further schisms which often resulted in individual families being torn apart. Emigration, whether by choice or necessity, was a major factor and the internecine struggles of the civil war saw terrible conflicts of loyalties as brother often fought brother. But the hope expressed by Friel here was to remain with him and to inform his writing throughout the Troubles.

Ulster and Donegal

It may be helpful at this point to clarify the situation regarding the geographical and political position of Donegal. When the Irish Free State was created in 1921 the old province of Ulster was split up. The six counties of

Antrim, Armagh, Down, Fermanagh, Derry (renamed Londonderry) and Tyrone became Northern Ireland (later to be incorporated into the United Kingdom) whilst the remaining three, Cavan, Donegal and Monaghan, were separated off and included in the new dominion. Sir Edward Carson, the Protestant leader of the Unionist Council, negotiated their exclusion because this was the only way a safe Protestant majority could be guaranteed. Partition isolated Donegal from the twenty-six other counties which make up the Republic of Ireland, to which it is attached by just a thread of land. (See the map on page 4, which shows the four provinces of Ireland, the border separating Northern Ireland from the Republic, the counties and real towns mentioned in the plays.)

The economy of the Irish Free State was drained by the civil war which resulted from Partition and Donegal, on the periphery of the new state, suffered even more from material deprivation. Neutrality during the Second World War, high trade tariffs and state censorship, led to economic and social apathy and, consequently, further isolation. The situation did not improve when Ireland became a republic in 1948. The whole of the country, and particularly the western counties, which include Donegal, remained trapped in a 1930s time-warp well into the 1950s and beyond. Friel's move to the Republic in the 1960s coincided with the introduction of vigorous and expansionist policies by the new Taoiseach, Sean Lemass, although the forces of reaction were still evident in the form of state censorship of literature and the continuing influence of the Catholic Church.

The majority of Friel's plays are set in Donegal in a mythical place called Ballybeg. The Irish name is Baile Beag, meaning 'small town', which suggests a cohesive community but could also be interpreted in the pejorative sense of a rigid and conservative mindset. 'Baile' also means 'home'. Donegal is a place of outstanding beauty, particularly its two-hundred-odd miles of dramatic coastline with spectacular cliffs and untrodden golden sands. In good weather it is easy to appreciate the winding roads, glens, lakes, rivers and rolling peatland; but when the winter rain lashes the pot-holed village streets, Donegal, once 'the edge of the known world', is a remote and even desolate place. Friel's sense of place is paramount to the setting and meaning of his plays. He returns to this location many times in periods ranging from the early nineteenth century to 'the present'. Ballybeg appears to remain the same, although in each play it is depicted on the verge of change, with its people constantly subjected to differing outside pressures which they either respond to or ignore.

Friel the Playwright

Friel believes that the writer is the voice of his people and over the years he has fulfilled this role with distinction. The various phases of his work have been informed always by a deep compassion for his fellow man and a profound understanding of human frailty. Friel is consistently inventive and unpredictable with form, but the content of his plays tends to explore recurrent themes. He has been drawn back many times to his memories, his family and his native place. Friel explains this using an image coined by his friend the poet Seamus Heaney: 'There are only certain stretches of ground over which the writer's divining rod will come to life' (Fintan O'Toole, 'Keeper of the Faith', *Guardian*, 16 June 1992, p. 26). The early plays, of which *Philadelphia, Here I Come!* is one, were 'all attempts at analysing different kinds of love' (Hickey and Smith, p. 222). He achieves this through explorations of familial relationships, the individual's connection with the community, the exile's attitude to home, and the power of real or imagined memory.

By the 1970s, despite considerable critical and popular success, Friel was prepared to abandon the theatre altogether and return to writing short stories. His dis-affection arose from what he perceived to be a lack of commitment in contemporary Irish theatre in comparison to its heyday when Synge (1871–1909) and O'Casey (1880–1964) gave voices of incomparable eloquence and vitality to, respectively, the dispossessed rural peasant and urban poor. Their work of uncompromising genius and unpalatable truth provoked riots in the theatre when national feelings were sensitive to criticism. Friel lamented the absence of such engagement on the contemporary scene from both playwrights and audiences. He main-tained that the future of the Irish drama 'must depend on the slow process of development of the Irish mind, and it will shape and be shaped by political events' ('Plays Peasant and Unpeasant', *Times Literary Supplement*, 17 March 1972, p. 306). Although he does not believe that 'art is the servant of any movement', the politics of Northern Ireland became the central focus of his work. Instead of turning from the theatre, he embarked on a new phase of writing, one which was more overtly political in intention. This included *The Freedom of the City*, which took the form of a drama documentary with material based on the official Inquiry that followed Bloody Sunday, when thirteen unarmed members of a civil rights march were shot dead by British paratroopers.

Although he never returned to this dramatic form it enabled him for the first time to examine the interpretation of historical 'facts' and the 'process' of history.

Friel's abiding concern with notions of history, myth and language reached its fullest expression in his masterpiece *Translations* and the companion piece *Making History*. These were the first and last of his plays to be produced by the Field Day Theatre Company that he founded with the actor Stephen Rea in 1980. The company was a cross-border initiative financed by the Arts Councils of both Northern Ireland and the Republic of Ireland which aimed to reach a broad constituency across the country and, when appropriate, abroad. Field Day was based in Derry, where it gave its inaugural production of *Translations*. The play has become a classic and its special qualities were immediately apparent at the première. Seamus Heaney recalls

> feeling that the energies awakened all over the country ... were indeed evidence of the power of theatre to do what Yeats said it might do: engross the present and dominate memory. The excitement which that play caused was palpable and its gratification had to do with a feeling that the dramatic form had allowed inchoate recognitions, both cultural and historical, to be clarified and comprehended. Most people talked about it with relish, some with resistance, all with awakened attention. (*The Times*, 5 December 1988, p. 18)

According to the *Irish Press*'s editorial, the première was 'in every sense a unique occasion with loyalists and nationalists, Unionists and SDLP, Northerners and Southerners laying aside their differences to join in applauding a play by a fellow Derryman, and one with a theme that is uniquely Irish.' That Friel and Field Day had touched a nerve was unquestionable. The people of Northern Ireland, and the citizens of Derry in particular, had lived through a decade of terror, but here was a play that used an historical setting to explore ideas that place the modern violence of Northern Ireland in a wider perspective, and by so doing was able to contribute to a positive understanding of the then current relations between Britain and Ireland. During this middle period, Friel perceived 'some kind of confidence' amongst Irish playwrights, 'who have no interest in the English stage. We are talking to ourselves as we must and if we are overheard in America or England, so much the better' (*Magill*, December 1980, p. 60). It is important to emphasise here that Friel is writing primarily for an Irish audience. That he has become a playwright of international stature is testament to the universal appeal and application of his themes despite, or perhaps because of, their dramatic location in the lives of small, closed communities.

At the end of *Translations* Hugh says, 'it is not the literal past, the "facts" of history, that shape us, but images of the past embodied in language' (p. 88). In *Making History* Friel demonstrates this point. *Making History* was Friel's final play for Field Day, in which Stephen Rea took the leading role of Hugh O'Neill, Earl of Tyrone, the sophisticated 'rebel' on whose 'history' the play is based. Here Friel shows the defeated O'Neill's life being 'translated' into a myth, the creation of a hero for the benefit of future generations of the Irish people. Rea observed that: 'History for the Irish is something that has not yet been completed because of the conflict we live in. Obviously if it can't be completed it has to be re-examined all the time, to find ways that we can move on.

The pleasing irony is that Friel is making his own version of history that is useful for us today, a history ... of reconciliation' (John Vidal, 'Stronger than fiction', *Guardian*, 5 December 1988, p. 36). As with *Translations*, this play is based on language, its power and limitations, and it is appropriate to note here Friel's skill in providing an individual voice for each character he creates. Idiosyncrasies, rhythms and patterns of speech, are all carefully selected and woven into the fabric of the text. Actors love the plays and trust what Friel writes.

In his later work Friel returns to the role of memory exemplifed in *Dancing at Lughnasa*. His preoccupation with language has developed into the possibility of eliciting and conveying meaning beyond words. In this glorious play, the power of both the physical and visual are given full expression through, respectively, the instrument of the actor's body and the plastic arts of the theatre. As I mentioned earlier, Friel has always been a formal innovator – the physical presentation of the 'divided-self', scenic time-shifts and 'flashbacks', the linguistic conceit of English as Irish, and so on. Friel's skill as a storyteller are clearly shown in his use of monologue, and in *Dancing at Lughnasa* he uses this form as a framing device for sequences of dialogue, dance and movement reinforced by potent visual imagery, emblematic properties and costume, evocative music and atmospheric lighting. The form is heightened poetic realism rooted in a specific society and time, but with a sense of the universal and eternal.

In addition to his original plays Friel has also adapted other writers, creating new versions of their work. These include two plays by Chekhov, with whom he is often compared. Both dramatists wrested poetry from everyday life and developed their own form of tragicomedy –

'laughter through tears'. The bittersweet *Dancing at Lughnasa* is a particularly good example. All Friel's plays are serious debates but they are infused with humour and irony. Perhaps the vision is still bleak, but the anger of the early plays has been replaced by the desire to heal. In celebration of Friel's seventieth birthday, his friend, playwright Thomas Kilroy wrote:

> As a writer he is a connoisseur of human failure. The vitality which makes the plays so widely loved, the music, the humour, the shared emotions, the sheer charm of the writing, is built over a dark perception of the human capacity to fail in all things, especially in the most important ones. The laughter and the dances, the moments of intimacy and love, the movement towards some kind of poise or grace at the end of the plays; all this is made even more precious by that shadow of imperfection which the Friel vision holds in place with unrelenting gaze. (*Irish Times*, 28 April 1999, p. 4)

Approach to Studying the Texts

We will now turn to the four plays to be considered in this volume in the order in which they were written. When dealing with Irish drama in general, and Friel's in particular, it is important to know something of the period in which the plays are set. This kind of detail is a given for an Irish audience, but for those not of that constituency I thought it helpful to contextualise all the plays with regard to their relevant historical, social and political background as appropriate. The map will also be of use here. However, after this basic introduction, as each play has its own distinctive form and features, the analytical approach will differ from text to text. We will always consider the stage-world, which includes a sense of place and the various scenographic elements, but the components of the dramatic structure will vary accordingly.

Because you only have access to the printed text, I am concerned that you are aware of the potential of the play in performance and I will, therefore, draw your attention at certain points to how the play 'works'. It is important that you always read Friel's stage-directions carefully because they provide so much information in this respect, and also try to visualise what is happening onstage, especially at key moments in the scenes. You should also consider the nature of the language Friel uses, and what goes on 'between the lines', in the pauses and the silences. This layer yields as much and sometimes more meaning than the surface text and will often be a pointer to a character's real intention, psychological disposition or emotional state. I hope that you will develop also a precise imaginative relationship to the locale, the communities and all the characters of the plays, those who appear and those who do not, through 'digging' for internal evidence in the texts. Friel makes this task enjoyable, as his plays are made up of a myriad of detail.

Friel uses Hiberno-English for some of the dialogue in several of the plays. This is an idiomatic form of the English language spoken by those whose ancestral tongue was Irish. It is strongest in Gaelic-speaking and rural districts and those parts of the country where Irish was spoken well into the mid-twentieth century. Donegal is such a place. Hence the different sentence constructions and, sometimes, unusual words that you will find in Friel's texts. For those of you who are not Irish there is absolutely no difficulty in understanding what is being said, particularly once you are used to the rhythms of the speech and familiar with the language's distinctive music. However, for further information on this subject you might like to consult Terence Patrick Dolan's *A Dictionary of Hiberno-English*, full details of which are given in the Bibliography.

Friel's plays are intensely theatrical, in the best sense of the word, rich in metaphor, with finely drawn characters and an extraordinary vitality which leaps off the page and the stage. Enjoy reading them but make every effort to see them in performance whenever an opportunity presents itself.

Philadelphia, Here I Come!

The Play

Philadelphia is set in 'the present', which means 1964, when it was first staged. The Republic of Ireland, even in the outreaches of County Donegal, has seen a considerable number of social and cultural changes over the last thirty years, which give some of the reference points in the play a definite 'period' feel. However, although emigration may not be such a prevalent fact of Irish life today, personal relationships and the significance of 'homeland' to the exiled individual are of enduring interest. These are areas which Friel himself defines as particularly important to an understanding of the play. 'I began *Philadelphia* in 1962 or '63. It was a play about an area of Irish life that I had been closely associated with in County Donegal. Our neighbours and our friends there have all been affected by emigration, but I don't think the play specifically concerns the question of emigration. *Philadelphia* was an analysis of a kind of love: the love between a father and a son and between a son and his birthplace' (Hickey and Smith, p. 222).

Friel's use of the word 'analysis' is revealing here. The play has no real plot. Things do happen, people come and go, and there is a story of sorts. But the overriding interest in the play is Gareth O'Donnell's internal struggle as he attempts to resolve the difficulties of his relationship with his father while he prepares to take the huge step of emigration and all that that implies. S. B. O'Donnell is a widower of many years who has withdrawn into himself, devoting all his time to his business – a general shop – and is now apparently incapable of expressing love. Moreover, he is a county councillor, a pillar of a community which appears to be stagnating – economically, socially, culturally and spiritually – from a combined lack of imagination and political will. Gareth is alienated from his father, the community and, if Ballybeg is a microcosm of Ireland, his country. *Philadelphia* explores this state of isolation and dislocation within a dramatic framework that maintains a delicate balance between naturalistic and non-naturalistic elements. The play's deeply serious intent is often expressed in richly comic terms but perhaps it is fuelled as much by anger as it is by love.

Historical Context

Nearly every Irish family knows of relatives living abroad, either those who have emigrated directly or the descendants of those who have emigrated. Emigration has had a profound effect upon Irish society, depopulating whole areas in Ireland and planting Irish communities mainly in the USA, Canada and Britain, but also in Australia and New Zealand.

As a result of the great tragedy of the Famine in 1845 about two million Irish citizens emigrated over the following ten years, approximately one-quarter of the entire population. This drastic measure was seen as the only way to escape the interminable poverty of life at home. Many landlords actually paid the passage money for their tenants to emigrate, as it seemed the only alternative to eviction, and a lot cheaper than maintaining a family on poor relief or keeping a man in the workhouse. Conditions on the transatlantic emigrant ships were appalling: over-crowding, primitive or non-existent sanitation, a limited supply of fresh water and poor food. Disease, therefore, was rampant and many deaths occurred during the voyages. However, contemporary accounts of the horrific suffering on board did not deter future emigrants, who had little or no choice but to make the dangerous voyage to a new life.

The Irish communities that were established in North America harboured fierce resentment against the land-lords and the English government, who were blamed for the catastrophe of the Famine and subsequent emigration. A strong sense of Irish nationalism grew in these communities and a great deal of Fenian activity in the 1860s onwards originated in the United States. During the Land War, hundreds of thousands of dollars were raised by the Land League in America to alleviate the peasants' suffering in the homeland; and from 1919 to 1921, funds were raised in the States to finance the new Irish Free State and the Irish Republican Army in their struggle against the British government.

There was a recession in the Irish Free State in the 1930s and, despite the fact that America was in the grip of a depression itself, a steady trickle of Irish emigrants looked to the New World for a new life. This is when the Sweeney family moved to Philadelphia. In the early 1960s America was still seen as a land of affluence and opportunity.

The Stage-World

Locale

This was the first play that Friel set in Ballybeg. The stage-directions are confined to the interior of the O'Donnell's home, but Friel gives us a wider picture of the environs through numerous references to places, people, events and other features of the locality: Mill Road, McLaughlin's Hotel, Loch na Cloc Cor, White Strand, caves, rocks, sea, fishing boats, farms, a football team, a carnival, a wake, the *Clarion* newspaper, Maggie Hanna, Neil McFadden, Charlie who owns the lorry, tinkers and so on.

However, despite the undoubted beauty of the landscape and the old-world charm of the village, life in Ballybeg is stultifying. The society is patriarchal, run by old men like S. B. O'Donnell, Master Boyle and Canon O'Bryne, but with a new breed of the establishment emerging represented here by the ambitious Senator Doogan; women are madonnas, dutiful wives, mothers, daughters or aunts; and young men resort to exaggerated stories of sexual conquest to fill the boredom of empty days. Jimmy Crerand, one of Gareth's friends – 'Best goalie we ever had' – has recently emigrated to America, another young life lost to the community (p. 59). Ballybeg is culturally impoverished and economically deprived – O'Donnell's business has shrunk, wages are meagre, bills are rarely paid and everybody knows everybody else's business. The trappings of Catholicism are much in evidence. Mass for all on Sundays (p. 57), grace before meals, and the Angelus and rosary is said daily in the O'Donnell household (pp. 72–4). The Church's attitude to sex is repressive. Gareth makes a joke of it: 'Steady, boy, steady. You know what the Canon says: long passionate kisses in lonely places ...' (p. 15). Gareth participates in these religious rituals but we know that his mind is elsewhere. His loss of faith is part of the condition, for there is no one to 'translate all this loneliness, this groping, this dreadful bloody buffoonery into Christian terms'. His final verdict is that Christianity is 'insane' (pp. 81–2).

America is an alternative world to that of Ballybeg. The image is distorted by Gareth's inclination to fantasise and Aunt Lizzy's disposition for loquacity. Gar's American heaven is full of great big sexy dames, downtown drive-ins, night clubs, Cadillacs, hamburgers, malted milk and slices of blueberry pie. The popular American song alluded to in the title of the play, and of which Gar sings snippets throughout, is the siren call of the New World which promises that women, money and success will be easily obtained. Aunt Lizzy describes a more quotidian world – although far removed from Gar's experience in Ballybeg – but with substantial material reward and job opportunities. The Sweeneys' success in America has not, however, brought them happiness – their life is empty without a child.

Setting

The play appears to be rooted in naturalism as the described setting would suggest, but the scenes are extremely atmospheric, and as the evening becomes night and then morning approaches the action takes on an almost dreamlike quality. Thus a form of heightened realism is achieved which appropriately accommodates Friel's poetic vision. This would be reinforced by the designer's use of colour, texture and, most important of all, lighting.

Friel indicates that the scene is revealed as '*the curtain rises*'. Curtains have been largely dispensed with in contemporary theatre but it is important to note when Friel indicates either a quick or slow curtain at the end of episodes or scenes. These instructions are in keeping with the rhythm of the scene that precedes the curtain, and whether it ends with a climax or ongoing action. The composite set combines the several locations required by the text and keeps the action moving. The kitchen is comfortless, '*a bachelor's kitchen*', no cloth on the table, '*rough cups and saucers*'. The bedroom is equally sparse and rudimentarily furnished – note the '*crockery jug and bowl*'. The O'Donnells' home is a cheerless place. Two important features stand out: the '*large school-type clock*' in the kitchen and the only nod to modernity, '*a record-player and records*', in the bedroom. Both of these have important functions to which we will return.

Other scenographic elements would relate to costume, props and sound. When Friel specifies an item of clothing it is bound to be significant, for example S. B. O'Donnell's attire. Apart from props used for general setting there are several which have particular resonance – the family suitcase, Kathy's photograph and Aunt Lizzy's letter. These simple objects trigger memories which have a profound effect on Gareth. Music emanates from the record-player. It ebbs and flows according to which room is in focus. Friel is specific here and the choice is crucial. Gareth plays Mendelssohn and ceilidh music – both powerful and moving but in entirely different ways. Gareth indulges in them in the relative safety of his 'survival shelter' – his bedroom. It is important, however, to determine when and why the music is being used. Another sound source may be the large clock on the kitchen wall relentlessly ticking away.

Dramatic Structure

In *Philadelphia*, Friel achieves a perfect marriage between content and form. Thus the structural devices of the divided self, time and memory are also thematic ideas. Here we will examine how these three elements are presented dramatically.

Divided self

The most innovative structural feature, which takes the play firmly beyond naturalism, is the division of the protagonist into a public persona and a private self. Friel states that Gar Public and Gar Private are two views of one man. Gar Public is presented to the world, varying his persona appropriately. Gar Private is his spirit, '*the man within, the conscience, the alter ego, the secret thoughts, the id*' (p. xi). All these descriptions define slightly different functions according to the situation in which Gar Public finds himself. It is important that although Gar Public can hear Gar Private, he cannot see him. Because the alter ego is embodied by an actor who we *can* see, it is easy to forget this simple fact. Notwithstanding that we as the audience are privy to Gar's most intimate thoughts, the split character also serves as a distancing device. Through Gar Private's interior monologue the audience is given a continuous commentary on the whole character's attitude and behaviour. We are provided with a double focus which enables us to both identify and sympathise, and yet remain intellectually engaged and critically aware.

We experience Gar Public as a warm, attractive, open, energetic, even passionate young man who can also be non-committal, taciturn and boorish. Gar Private is sensitive, witty, sardonic, outrageous and admonitory. It is Gar Private who articulates what Gar Public cannot or dare not. Gar Private is Gar Public's potential, what he could become with the right support and understanding. Together they represent a wholeness. But although Gar Private is freer, either cajoling Gar Public to act decisively or warning him against his excesses, the reality of Ballybeg and a life which is loveless and doomed to failure constantly reasserts itself. In a sense Gar O'Donnell is already in exile, there is no place for him in Ballybeg and yet he is desperate to retain a positive memory of his birthplace. He spends the whole play attempting to do this, but at the last is denied the most meaningful memory of all.

Friel establishes Gar Public first in a short sequence with Madge in the opening scene of the play. As he moves into the bedroom singing, 'Philadelphia, here I come, rightah backah where Ah started from – ', he is joined in the first half of the song by an offstage voice (p. 3). As he lies on the bed in characteristic position, the dialogue goes:

PUBLIC: It's all over.
PRIVATE: (*off, in echo-chamber voice*) And it's all about to begin. It's all over.
PUBLIC: And all about to begin.

The echo-chamber effect suggests an 'otherness', disembodied, unworldly. Thus as Gar Private is introduced the naturalistic mode is broken. This heightened moment is sustained through the first exchange by the pattern of speech and the quality of sound, the two combining to imply that Gar O'Donnell is in some kind of purgatory. It is in this limbo between ending and beginning that Gar's condition is explored.

The mode and mood break as Gar Private is physicalised onstage. The word 'think' is a bridge into Gar Public/ Gar Private's first routine. There is a hesitancy which surrounds the word, suggesting that this is a very dangerous thing to do, but for the time being Gar Private evades the issue by entering into one of his fantasies. Gar has a full repertoire of these flights of fancy, or 'antics' as Madge calls them, and Friel introduces several of them in this opening sequence – fighter pilot, football hero, pop singer and military prisoner 'condemned' by his own decision to emigrate to America (pp. 3–5). Note that Gar Private disparagingly describes Ireland as 'the land of the curlew and the snipe, the Aran sweater and the Irish sweepstakes' – clichéd images beloved of the Irish Tourist Board. It is clear from the start, therefore, that Gar has a fertile imagination, evidenced by these racy routines which reveal a vivid inner life.

The 'double-act' is also a useful means of exposition. Friel imparts a few details of Gar's personal history in the sequence that follows the first brief encounter with his father (pp. 8–10). Gar's failure to complete his university education is here flippantly dismissed, but becomes a subject of self-admonishment later in the play. Towards the end of this passage Friel introduces an oft-repeated refrain used by both Gar Public and Gar Private: 'It is now sixteen or seventeen years since I saw the Queen of France, then the Dauphiness, at Versailles; and surely never lighted on this orb, which she hardly seemed to touch, a more delightful vision.' These are the opening

23

lines of Edmund Burke's *Reflections on the Revolution in France*, written in 1790, which was essentially a defence of the *ancien régime*. Burke was an eighteenth-century Irish statesman and philosopher whose European reputation rested on this book which, on a purely realistic level, Gar may well have come across in his discussions with Master Boyle or in his first year at university. On a literary level, provided the reference is known to the audience, the quotation can be seen as an ironic comment by Gar on his own 'rebellion' against the conservatism of Ballybeg and, by extension, Ireland. Hence his flight from the homeland. However, I am sure that most members of the audience unfamiliar with Burke's writings will respond to it on a dramatic level. Used frequently, it becomes a kind of mantra that Gar resorts to at moments of pressure, when he is in some difficulty or distress. You can look for these occasions to see how and why the quotation is being employed and by which Gar.

The device of the public and private self is also a source of comedy and, indeed, many of the sequences are very funny. In addition to the verbal wit and neatly executed impersonations there is also a considerable amount of physical humour, all of which requires virtuoso playing from the two actors. However, as you will have seen, Gar's moods and responses can turn on a sixpence or, occasionally, there is a slower shift from one emotional state to another. These moments, which we shall examine later, can be poignant or deeply moving. Comedy can be counterpointed by tragedy or tragedy can be undercut by comedy within a scene or even a speech. I referred to this mix or juxtaposition of forms in the Introduction, and you will find many examples in this play.

Friel, mainly through the split character of Gar, also

employs irony as a dramatic method. Gar is still singing 'Philadelphia, here I come!' at the end of Episode One, but with less exuberance and seemingly with a need to convince himself that his decision to emigrate is the right one.

Time

The action of the play is presented in a series of short scenes divided into three Episodes which mark the passage of time from seven o'clock in the evening through to the '*small hours of the morning*' of the following day. This linear structure accommodates the events of the play set in the present. There are numerous references to time: people ask or check the time, O'Donnell winds the clock, Private's sardonic 'tick-tock' during the meal, Gar's repeated reminder to himself that he is leaving at 7.15 a.m., and so on. Time in Ballybeg is leaden, endured by engaging in meaningless rituals. To begin with the action appears to be played almost in real time, but as Gar's impending departure looms ever nearer there is an acceleration of time which exerts a tremendous pressure on Gareth to make peace with his father and to come to terms with his loss.

The past has a constant bearing on the present. Two scenes move backwards in time showing events of the past physically manifest onstage. They are linked by Kathy. In the first Gar recalls his humiliating encounter with Senator Doogan. It is important in not only showing the termination of Gar's relationship with Kathy and a good reason for him to leave Ballybeg, but also introduces the wider issue of class. Gar is not considered a socially acceptable husband for Kathy by the ambitious Doogan; the medical student, the professional man with prospects, would make the more advantageous marriage and is, therefore, preferred. In the scene, Public capitulates before the Senator but, on reflection, Private delivers a satirical indictment of the man: 'You know, of course, that he carries one of those wee black cards in the inside pocket of his jacket, privately printed for him: "I am a Catholic. In case of accident send for a bishop." And you know, too, that in his spare time he travels for maternity corsets; and that he's a double spy for the Knights and the Masons; and that he takes pornographic photographs of Mrs D. and sends them anonymously to reverend mothers' (p. 22).

The second flashback takes place on Kathy's wedding day, when Gar receives a visit from the Sweeneys and their friend Ben Burton. In his demoralised state, Gar is vulnerable to Aunt Lizzy's overtures to become her substitute son. Here Public makes the impetuous decision to emigrate – as Private says to Public: 'She got you soft on account of the day it was, didn't she?' The placing of the scene early on in Episode Two allows us to assess all that follows in the light of how and why the decision was taken. Both scenes are useful distancing devices – we are involved with Gar's predicament but we are also able to stand back and consider cause as well as effect.

Gareth is also projected forward into an imagined future in America through his fantasies, presented in a series of amusing, highly theatrical monologues or duologues. Thus events in the past, present and future are all brought to bear on Gareth's dilemma in his last hours in Ballybeg.

Memory
Philadelphia has been described as a memory play, and indeed the power of memory, either real or imagined, is an important theme. We have already seen how recollec-

tions of the past are built into the play's structure but memories – retained, recalled or returned unbidden – recurrently echo across the pattern of action. Private recognises how the imagination filters memory: '... but what it was all about you can't remember, can you? Just the memory of it – that's all you have now – just the memory; and even now, even so soon, it is being distilled of all its coarseness; and what's left is going to be precious, precious gold ...' (p. 66). This is what Gareth will remember of his escapades with Ned, Tim and Joe. However, other memories are more problematical.

Early in Episode One Madge gives Public his clean clothes to pack, bringing with her a suitcase and some rope to secure it (pp. 5–6). Madge and Public are both preoccupied and the suitcase is left on the floor, forgotten. After a sharp encounter with his father (the first time they are seen together in the play), Public returns to his packing to the strains of the second movement of Mendelssohn's violin concerto. It is important to remember that the music is playing throughout the following sequence (pp. 10–12). If you have not already done so, it would be helpful to listen to it to fully appreciate the effect it has in supporting the mood and emotional current of the scene. Public discovers the faded newspaper, lifts it out of the case reading the name and date. But it is Private who recognises its significance – the suitcase has not been used since his parents' honeymoon in Bundoran.

Public cannot cope with the emotional intensity of this moment. He resorts to prayer, hiding his feelings in the comforting ritual. It is Private who articulates the tender memory of his mother, Maire, passed on to him by Madge. His lyrical language reflects his feelings for her, his sense of loss, and the femininity and grace of this spirited young girl from Bailtefree who liked to run barefoot in the countryside. It also captures the poignancy of her secret regret that she had married, too young, a man too old. Madge's telling also reveals something of O'Donnell which Private acknowledges here: Maire had thought he was the 'grandest gentleman that ever lived', that 'he must have known' – and Friel repeats the phrase for emphasis – that she was unhappy as he listened to her 'many a night ... crying herself to sleep', and that maybe it was a blessing that she had died three days after giving birth to Gar. As Private speaks, Public carefully puts the newspaper inside a shirt and packs it in the suitcase. Thus the burden of the past goes with him into exile. There is an illustration of the old suitcase on the front cover of Faber's published text – an appropriate image from the play and even more resonant when you know all that the suitcase contains.

But for Gareth the most important memory of all is of a fishing trip with his father. He has full sensory recall of a particular moment when he sat in a blue boat in a state of complete happiness and companionable silence with his father, who sang a song because he was happy too. It is not until the final scene that Gareth screws up the courage to ask his father if he also remembers. O'Donnell does not (p. 91). But there is a double irony here. O'Donnell also has a memory of Gareth in a sailor suit refusing one morning to go to school because he wanted instead to go into his 'daddy's business'. Madge denies that Gareth had a sailor suit but O'Donnell insists on the truth of his memory (p. 93). We will return to these scenes later when we examine the relationship between Gareth and his father in more detail, and the significance of memory to the play as a whole.

Language

Friel uses a wide range of language in the play: from the standard Irish/English of the educated and/or middle-class characters to a Hiberno-English idiom for the Ballybeg natives which varies in degree according to character, with some examples of demotic speech from Gareth and 'The Boys'. Each character has his or her own speech pattern and rhythm, and some have idiosyncratic phrases or words. Public and Private employ different modes of speech and accents in their impersonations which Friel indicates in his stage-directions and are easy, therefore, to identify. It is for Private, however, that Friel creates a more poetic form. The lyrical evocation of memories of his mother and his childhood, recreated through the power of his own imagination, are magical moments in the play.

One of the most important and powerful features of language in the play, and easily missed when reading, is Friel's use of silence. The failure of the relationship between father and son is the result of a failure of communication. The silence which Gareth once shared with his father was one of companionship and was counterpointed in both their memories by chatter and laughter. This is no longer the case. Silence is 'the enemy', a recognition that father and son no longer have anything to say to each other. There are several examples of extended sequences where the silence 'speaks' of failure and despair. There are also instances where the surface text is filled with dialogue – usually Private's monologues – but where, beneath or between the lines, the characters are existing in a silent world. This applies particularly to O'Donnell, who has very few lines and only one speech of any length in the whole play. It is what he does not say that is significant and you should not underestimate the power of his silent physical presence on stage.

Characters and Relationships

We will now consider the characters and their relationship to Gareth. As we examine the various encounters between Gareth and those most closely involved in his life in Ballybeg, we will see how more of Gareth's dilemma is revealed and analysed.

S. B. O'DONNELL

Episode One: The relationship between father and son is at the heart of the play. It is a while before we see S. B. O'Donnell but we learn a fair amount about him in Public's conversations with Madge. O'Donnell is mean – making Gareth work on his last day at home even into overtime – and Gareth is afraid of him. Madge's dead-pan 'That flattened him' in response to Public's consciously self-deprecating description of how he 'handled' the situation acknowledges this (p. 3). O'Donnell's mind is on business even during the Angelus (p. 3) – we hear later that he opens every day until seven o'clock except Saturday when closing time is midnight – but he appears to pay his son a pitiful wage, less than Madge. On Gareth's last day at home O'Donnell has made no mention of his leaving. Madge tries to comfort Public with the thought that 'just because he doesn't say much doesn't mean that he hasn't feelings like the rest of us ... He said nothing either when your mother died.' Madge also confides that O'Donnell slept very little the previous night, interpreting this as the sign of a troubled mind (pp. 6–7).

Gar's first encounter with his father is short and sharp. Friel tells us how O'Donnell is [over]dressed, denoting his concern to appear responsible and respectable, an almost Victorian figure. Friel also succinctly describes the two different reactions in response to O'Donnell's command-ing call – '*Public reacts instinctively. Private keeps calm.*' But ultimately '*Instinct is stronger than reason: Public rushes to his door and opens it*' (p. 7). We now see a very different Gar Public, one who shows '*a surly, taciturn gruffness*' in speech and gesture, his habitual demeanour when in the company of his father. We also see that in direct confrontation with him Public is unable to think clearly – he becomes confused and incoherent. O'Donnell gives no quarter, his dismissive 'Agh!' says it all. It is interesting to look at this sequence in the light of a subsequent passage which we have touched on earlier, in the section on memory (pp. 11–12). Here O'Donnell is seen through the eyes of Gar's mother as a resplendent gentleman, and he in turn is captivated by his young bride – 'he couldn't take his eyes off her'. There would seem to have been a mutual attraction and, when Maire perhaps begins to regret her marriage, O'Donnell is sensitive to her distress. At the end of this sequence we also learn that Maire died as a result of Gareth's birth (p. 12). How guilty does Gareth feel about this? How far does O'Donnell blame his son for the loss of his beautiful young wife? Neither man articulates his feelings – although Gar Private falters when referring to her death, rapidly changing the subject and the mood (p. 12). O'Donnell only mentions his wife to Madge: 'I was too old for her, Madge, eh?' (p. 93).

We never know fully what 'S. B.' stands for. Boyle and the Canon address O'Donnell as Sean; otherwise, for the most part, he is referred to by his surname. Gar 'translates' the initials as 'Screwballs', his pet name for his father, among others. We see them together next in an extended sequence (pp. 26–31). Private's witty commentary on O'Donnell's '*ponderous*' actions as he emerges from the shop for his tea is extremely funny. The numbing drabness of his father's nightly routine is a kind of torture for Gareth who, instead of screaming aloud, internalises his irritation. In dramatic terms the mundanity of the father's ritual is contrasted with the inspired invention of the son's monologue. The two men's exchange is perfunctory – 'Now for a little free conversation. But no obscenities, Father dear; the child is only twenty-five' – the formality of the meal broken only by O'Donnell removing his teeth – 'Ah! That's what we were waiting for; complete informality; total relaxation between intimates.' But of course they are no such thing, and this unthinking but gross gesture on O'Donnell's part prompts Gareth, in the guise of his Private self, to articulate his anger and despair. Friel's stage-directions indicate that '*all trace of humour fades*' and that Private becomes '*more and more intense and it is with an effort that he keeps his voice under control*'. Here is a very good example of moving from a comic to a more serious tone.

Private lists his grievances, which are all well-founded, but he is at his most perceptive when he identifies the crux of their problem – '*we embarrass one another*' (the italics are Friel's). They are incapable of expressing any compassion, understanding or love towards each other. Private does not use the word 'love' – in fact it is a word rarely used in the play – but this is what he means. Gareth yearns for his father to ask him to stay, willing him to say it. Private's 'Say it! Say it! Say it!' erupts into the scene as a roar from Public to Madge for help. Public turns his anguished cry into a request for bread and he stumbles from the room (pp. 28–9). Because we have been listening to Private's tirade it is easy to forget that father and son have been sitting eating their meal in virtual silence. Friel draws our attention to this by Madge's ironic observation: 'The chatting in this place would deafen a body. Won't the house be quiet soon enough – long enough?' (p. 29), and her further caustic remark: 'A body couldn't get a word in edgeways with you two!' (p. 30) – both of which are also prompts to O'Donnell to speak to his son properly before his departure. O'Donnell does pay Public his wages but their joyless exchange provokes a wild harangue from Private in the form of a 'confession' that he may be a sex-maniac. There is an air of desperation about this, as though he is trying to shock his father, but because the 'secret' is never spoken or shared it is a pathetic gesture.

Episode Two: Gareth and his father do not appear together in Episode Two but we, and Gar, learn more about the O'Donnells' marriage from Aunt Lizzy. She never completes her rambling account of the wedding in Bailtefree chapel but Lizzy does say in passing, 'But he was good to her. I'll say that for S. B. O'Donnell' (p. 46). She also points out the difference between her family and her brother-in-law's: 'That was always the kind of us Gallagher girls, wasn't it ... either laughing or crying ... you know, sorta silly and impetuous, shooting our big mouths off, talking too much, not like the O'Donnell's – you know – kinda cold –' (p. 50). Aunt Lizzy's judgement has a profound effect on Gar. Public does not heed Private's warning of 'Don't man, don't', and impetuously declares that he wants to go to America. Gar cannot bear to be thought an O'Donnell, 'cold like'. This lack of warmth may be genetic, a family characteristic, but O'Donnell's inability to show any affection towards his son is also the result of life experience. Gareth seems to have inherited his mother's anarchic spirit, manifest to us in the character of Gar Private, and, despite his apparent kindness towards Maire, O'Donnell may have found it impossible to satisfy her sexually. This is implied in a brief passage between Gareth and Madge to which we will return.

There is also in Episode Two a brief but important passage between Madge and O'Donnell relevant to the father and son relationship (p. 54). O'Donnell enters from the shop with a newspaper and sits at the top of the table opposite Gar's room. Madge watches him read for a while and then, close to tears, strongly accuses him of his lack of consideration towards her. Madge has the courage to do what Gar cannot – confront O'Donnell with his inadequacy and insensitivity. Madge's distress is possibly heightened by her concern for Gareth, for she knows that he is also a victim of O'Donnell's neglect and indifference. O'Donnell is perplexed by her outburst. Friel says that he 'stares after her, then out at the audience' as if searching for some kind of meaning in her behaviour. However, there follows a significant sequence conveyed entirely by physical means and played in complete silence. O'Donnell is preoccupied, he cannot read. All his movements are executed 'very slowly' and, although described in a few lines, take up a considerable amount of stage-time. The sequence has both weight and purpose. O'Donnell 'sighs' before getting up and moving slowly back into the shop. What is he thinking? It would strike a false note at this

point if Friel provided a speech for O'Donnell to
articulate his feelings; the silence is more eloquent. The
physical image epitomises failure. Here the playwright
shifts the balance of sympathy towards O'Donnell who,
at this moment, appears old, tired and as isolated as Gar.

Episode Three, Part One: Episode Three starts with the
family at prayer. As the rosary is said, Private's fictional
narrative looks to his future life in America with himself
as the central 'character'. Here he is 'The Bachelor', 'a
man without intimates, something of an enigma',
consumed with passion for the daughter of an exiled
Russian prince and so on (p. 73). His reverie is interrupted
by Madge when they reach his decade. As he returns to
his musing the mood changes, Private breaks from his
position and stands looking down intently on his father.
The focus is fully on Private as he asks his father if
'behind those dead eyes and that flat face are there
memories of precious moments in the past?' Private tells
of *his* precious memory sitting in the old blue boat
wearing his father's hat and coat, 'just the two of us
fishing on a lake on a showery day' (p. 74). He recalls his
'great, great happiness' and 'bubbling joy' as they sat in
silence – not the oppressive silence, 'the enemy' of now –
but an easy mutual sharing of a blissful moment; and
then, the father's song which Private softly sings. In the
two halves of Private's monologue he moves from the
ridiculous to the sublime. The memory is achingly
beautiful in the simplicity of its expression, and powerfully evoked by Friel in ironic contrast to the 'somnolent
drone' of the mechanical prayers in the background. His
longing to know if his father remembers too gives Public
the courage to broach the subject of the 'aul boat on

Lough na Cloc Cor', but the Canon's entrance interrupts any possible response from O'Donnell (pp. 75–6).

During the game of draughts, Private returns to the memory (p. 83). He is in an agitated state and in a moment of inspiration Public puts on the second movement of the Mendelssohn in an attempt to reach his father emotionally. As the music plays Private tells his father how 'a great beauty' that happened when he was a boy on an afternoon in May has become a memory that haunts him, because he no longer knows whether it really happened or whether he imagined it. He desperately wants it to have happened, he needs his father to verify that it happened, but the father and son – 'each of us is all the other has' – no longer communicate, no longer even look at each other. Although Private is inches away from his father he is, of course, only speaking to him in his imagination, Public remaining in his bedroom in a state of uncertainty and anguish.

In one of the rare moments that Gareth is absent from the scene (although still onstage in the bedroom), O'Donnell talks of him to the Canon (p. 84). 'All he asks is to sit in there and play them records all day ... Terrible man for the records', is his verdict on his son. However, unbeknown to Gareth, his father is more than aware of the enormity of the step he is taking: '... tomorrow morning. Powerful the way time passes, too'. The scene between O'Donnell and the Canon ends on an ambivalent note (p. 85). Is this about Madge? The Canon certainly thinks so. For O'Donnell, however, there may be other resonances.

Episode Three, Part Two: The final part of the play opens with the visual image of Gar's suitcases outside the bedroom door with his coat, cap and envelope containing X-ray and visa lying across them. O'Donnell cannot sleep. Again the silent physicalisation is eloquent. He goes over to the suitcases and touches the coat before sitting at the table where he stares at Gar's bedroom door (p. 85). As father and son meet unexpectedly they continue to evade any intimacy, despite the lateness of the hour and the imminence of Gar's departure. Public talks of practicalities, Private urges him to speak of the memory. Public gains in confidence through the following exchange, resulting almost in a reversal of roles (pp. 87–9). The focus of their conversation is on the running of the shop. It is obvious that Public knows exactly 'what's what'. He takes on an authority previously absent and O'Donnell is the one who has to ask for confirmation or give assurances that things will be attended to. The passage also retrospectively reveals details of their daily lives, a kind of summary of how they have rubbed along together all these years, and serves as a transition into the climactic or, as it transpires, anti-climactic moment of the memory. The turning point is O'Donnell inadvertently referring to 'a Yank coming home ...' (p. 89). In the pause that follows, both men are deciding whether to broach the subject of Gareth's departure. Public is oblique in his approach by suggesting that he needs the pills to get a few hours sleep, but leaves the rest unsaid. His father, however, refers directly to Gar's journey. He can only offer banalities about the weather and advice on the safest part of the aircraft to sit in. He tries to distance these concerns from himself by emphasising that the advice was offered by the Canon, but this only serves to show that beneath the apparent indifference there is real anxiety, perhaps even fear, for his son and what he is about to experience (pp. 89–90). Finally, Private persuades Public to speak, but now there is another kind of fear: 'Now! Now! He might remember – he might. But if he does, my God, laddo – what if he does?' If his father remembers, will this make it harder to leave?

A subtle change has taken place during the course of the play. All the boisterous optimism that Gareth showed at the beginning has changed to a trepidation that what he might be going to is no better than what he is leaving. In fact, his birthplace means more to him than he realised. Early in Episode Two Private says, 'You know what you're doing, don't you, laddybuck? Collecting memories and images and impressions that are going to make you bloody miserable; and in a way that's what you want, isn't it?' (pp. 40–1); and later, when regretting his moment of weakness with Aunt Lizzy, Private observes, '(*quietly, deliberately*) You don't want to go, laddybuck. Admit it. You don't want to go' (p. 53). Each time, Public evades the issue. Towards the end of Episode Two he protests too much in his encounter with Kathy: 'All this bloody yap about father and son and all this sentimental rubbish about "homeland" and "birthplace" – yap! Bloody yap!' – and her words, 'It isn't as bad as that, Gar.' begin to haunt him (p. 69). If he leaves Ballybeg, will he be losing something rare? In the closing moments of the episode, Public calls to his father in a *'whispered shout'*, 'Screwballs, say something! Say something, father!' (p. 71). It is significant that Public articulates this need – before, it was Private who insisted, 'Say it! Say it! Say it!' and Public who avoided the confrontation.

Now Gareth is faced with the possibility that his father might share his memory. If his father does remember, will that make up for all the years of lovelessness and disappointment? Will the failure that he feels he has inherited become more bearable and in time be expiated? The moment has come when he must know. Public speaks *'with pretended carelessess'*, O'Donnell is *'confused, on guard'*, but slowly, agonisingly, the truth emerges that his father does not remember. Look carefully at the tone of this sequence: Public's anxious questioning, O'Donnell's confused response, with Private's mocking laughter undercutting both, their respective energies providing three different rhythms which combine to create a dissonance (pp. 90–2). This is Gareth's waking nightmare from which he cannot escape. Of course, he attempts to by rushing out into the shop, but he will carry this knowledge with him wherever he goes. O'Donnell cannot remember the blue boat or the song, nor can he see beyond his son's questions to what might motivate them – he lacks the necessary sensitivity and understanding.

However, something has stirred within him. When Madge returns, O'Donnell politely asks about the baby but his mind is still on Gareth. He needs first to convince himself that he will manage without his son. This he does, acknowledging at the same time the dwindling fortunes of his business. Then something quite unexpected happens. He recalls in vivid detail, and with delight, a memory of Gar as a little boy in a sailor suit – note how definitely he brushes aside Madge's objection – in which he and his son were 'happy as larks' together. The obvious pride and affection he felt for his son – 'and him as manly looking, and this wee sailor suit as smart looking on him' – has been crystallised in this image. But it has remained locked inside him all his life, along with his ability to articulate his love. For this brief moment, Friel allows O'Donnell's imagination to soar, giving him a voice and a language which we would not have expected. Friel also provides him with a touching insight at the end of the speech: 'Maybe, Madge, maybe it's because I could have been his grandfather, eh?' (p. 93). To this and the question about his wife, Madge has no answer – 'They're a new race – a new world' (p. 94). O'Donnell is a figure from another age. As he leaves the stage he takes his memory and his unanswered questions with him: 'In the wee sailor suit – all the chatting he used to go through ... I don't know either ...' (p. 94). O'Donnell is presented for the most part as a character whose predictability is a reflection of his rigid attitudes and a source of irritation to his son. In these moments of unpredictability, Friel shows us a sympathetic side to O'Donnell's character. Not only does this support Madge's view of O'Donnell and make more credible his marriage to Maire, but we in the audience are forced at this late stage to reassess our response to him.

MADGE

Madge is a wonderful creation, totally believable as a human being and yet used by Friel as a kind of choric figure throughout the play. Madge sees most things and by a nudge here and a word there tries to maintain a semblance of civility in the household. Of the same generation as O'Donnell she understands the world that shaped him, but unlike O'Donnell – whom she calls 'the Boss' – Madge is more tolerant of change. Her down-to-earth attitude and sense of irony show a sure grip on reality and it is always to Madge that Gareth turns for help. Madge and Gar Public start and end the play. At the beginning, Public is in a state of euphoria, full of optimism, looking forward to a new life. His relationship with Madge is easy and intimate: despite her struggles he insists on waltzing with her and, eventually, elicits the response he wants from her – yes, she will miss him. Madge knows, however, that Gareth is upset, and uses irony against him to deflect the hurt – 'He's losing a treasure, indeed!' (p. 2). When he affects 'indifference' towards his father, she retorts with like – 'Your tea's on the table – but that's a matter of total indifference to me.' (p. 6).

It is through Madge that Gareth learns about his mother. It is, of course, probable that Gar romanticises the image that Madge passes on to him, but she is loyal to Maire's memory, refusing to be drawn when he becomes curious about his mother's affairs: 'I've told you before: she went with a dozen – that was the kind of her – she couldn't help herself ... And any other nosing about you want to do, ask the Boss. For you're not going to pump me' (p. 80). Madge has no time, however, for Aunt Lizzy. When the Sweeneys are visiting, Madge refuses to look at them, her face *'tight with disapproval'* (p. 47), but as she takes her silent farewell of Gareth she softens a little: 'That Lizzy one'll look after him well, I suppose, if she can take time off from blatherin' ... Never had much time for blatherin' women ...' (p. 94). She is equally disapproving of 'The Boys'. Her displeasure is informed by the casual way they are treating Gar's departure. Unbeknown to him, she has even invited them to tea so that at least an appearance of friendship is maintained. But the boys, despite their jocular banter, are disrespectful and her thoughtful gesture backfires (pp. 56–7).

Madge is the buffer between father and son. She tries to explain O'Donnell's behaviour to Gar although she recognises his shortcomings. I have already drawn your attention to Madge's unexpected outburst at O'Donnell

(p. 54); then we were looking at the passage to show O'Donnell's incomprehension, but consider it now with Madge as the main focus. She accuses him, *'on the point of tears'*, of not treating her like 'a lady'; in fact when *'the tears begin to come'*, it is evident that he treats her like a skivvy. Madge realises that she is not appreciated. Gareth, on the other hand, knows her worth. The exchange between Madge and Public about the Mulhern children is revealing. She shows her *'shy delight'* at the possibility that the new baby might be named after her and, even though she is fully stretched at the O'Donnells', she will still find time to help Nelly out on Sunday. It is Private who comments: 'And now what are you sad about? Just because she lives for those Mulhern children, and gives them whatever few half-pence she has? Madge, Madge, I think I love you more than any of them. Give me a piece of your courage, Madge.' (p. 25). Of course, we learn later that the baby has been named Brigid. Madge tries it out and, philosophically, agrees that it sounds better: 'Madge Mulhern – I don't know – it's too aul'-fashioned or something ...' (p. 94). You will see that she tries to resolve this hurt shortly after her exchange with O'Donnell about 'a new race – a new world'. Madge understands that things move on and painful experiences are there to be endured.

Madge's musing about the name is contained within a soliloquy. We are used to Gar Public talking to himself in the guise of Gar Private but this dramatic method for another character is a new departure. However, when played it seems to arise quite naturally from the heart of the action. Madge is very tired and she is literally talking to herself as she sorts through Gareth's things. She knows that he will be 'in grief' for several weeks at leaving home, but prompted by the appearance of the apple – a nice human touch – comforts herself with the thought that he will be 'all right'. From the beginning of the play we have been made aware of Madge's feet. In the stage-directions Friel states that she walks *'as if her feet were precious'* (p. 1); and Public calls her 'aul fluke-feet' as we hear her *'flapping'* across the kitchen (p. 40). This slight physical impediment gives rise to some humour, but at the end of the play Friel uses it to show Madge's generosity of spirit. She puts £2 in an envelope into Gar's coat: 'That'll get him a cup of tea on the plane. I had put them two pounds by me to get my feet done on the fair day. But I can wait till next month. From what I hear, there's no big dances between now and then ...' (p. 94). Madge's conscious use of irony in the punchline prevents the thought and gesture from becoming sentimental.

Madge silently *'raises her hand in a sort of vague Benediction'* towards where she believes Gar to be in his bedroom. But as she *'shuffles'* to the scullery she recalls that the father was much like the son at his age, 'leppin, and eejtin' about and actin' the clown; as like as two peas'; and anticipates that the son will 'turn out just the same'. Her conclusion is a bleak one: 'And although I won't be here to see it, you'll find that he's learned nothin' in-between times. That's people for you – they'd put you astray in the head if you thought long enough about them' (p. 94).

Madge and Public share the last scene. He seems composed – remember we last saw him rushing out of his father's presence. He also appears to have tidied and washed up. Madge will not reveal her disappointment at being denied the simple pleasure of having the baby named after her or that she has just been talking to his father, and evades answering Gar Public's questions directly. He senses a resistance but, not wanting to trouble him, she states simply, 'If there was something wrong, wouldn't I tell you?' (p. 95). Private agrees: 'Of course she would. Who else has she?' This thought is echoed by Madge a few lines later. Public asks her, 'you'd let me know if – if he got sick or anything?' to which she responds, 'Who else would there be?' (p. 95). Both Public and Private watch Madge *shuffle off* as Private tries to record in his mind the film he will 'run over and over again'. Private repeats her name and then asks Public why he has to leave. The ambivalence of the ending is disturbing as Friel leaves Gareth's dilemma unresolved.

MASTER BOYLE

Friel gives a detailed description of Master Boyle's physical appearance and mannerisms – a striking figure despite his shabbiness. It is important to note that O'Donnell is '*barely courteous*' towards him. The reason for this emerges later: Maire. Private's thoughts are also interesting: 'God but he's a sorry wreck too, arrogant and pathetic. And yet whatever it is about you ...' (p. 31). This unfinished thought hangs in the air, suggesting that Gar has some sympathy with Boyle. The row between Boyle and the Canon appears to be a regular occurrence. Boyle seems to approve of Gar's decision to emigrate, to get out of Ballybeg and experience 'Impermanence and anonymity' in America, although the phrase has a hollow ring. The boast of the appointment he has been offered in Boston is clearly a fabrication. Boyle seems fond of Gareth, remembers the gifts, gives him the poems and, although he tells him to forget Ballybeg and Ireland, asks Gareth to write to him from Philadelphia and to look out for publishing opportunities for him in America. But he has to retain his intellectual superiority by reminding Gar of his 'average intelligence'. He is not, however, above touching his former pupil for ten shillings (50p) and takes the offered £1 note without looking at it.

Gareth is in some difficulty here. He is aware throughout the scene that Boyle could have been his father. Private proffers the unspoken question about Maire, 'did you love her?' (p. 33). Boyle recalls knowing all the Gallagher girls 'in the past' but he does repeat Maire's name, adding 'your mother'; but leaves the rest of the thought unexpressed (p. 34). Their exchange is fragmented. Boyle, who is driving the conversation, is incapable of sustaining a thought for any length of time. This is clearly the result of his drinking which, Madge confirms later, started after Maire broke off the affair (p. 80). Upset by his public humiliation, concerned not to bump into the Canon, and in desperate need of a drink, Boyle's anxiety tips over into a brief emotional display as he embraces Gar Public. Boyle seems genuinely upset, his final words being, 'I'll miss you, Gar' – perhaps he is losing his last link with Maire (p. 35). Public is deeply disturbed by the incident while Private urges him to get a grip on himself: 'He's nothing but a drunken aul schoolmaster – a conceited, arrogant wash-out.' He is indeed all of these, but he has shown an affection for Gar which has been denied him elsewhere, and from Public's response it would seem the feeling is reciprocated. Certainly Boyle returns to Gar's thoughts later in the play (p. 80).

THE BOYS
Friel's stage-directions are very full in describing the physical aspects of the scene with 'The Boys' and helpful

in differentiating between the three of them. The scene explores their limited horizons and demonstrates their various attitudes towards Gar's departure. Friel is also specific about Gar's mood and how it changes during the course of the scene; the suggestion that '*he is already spiritually gone from them*' is significant. The meeting with the boys is important to Gar – these are his peers, his friends. He is initially flattered that they have come for him, but as they persistently refuse to acknowledge his departure he becomes isolated rather than the centre of attention. Look carefully at their 'conversation'; they are not really communicating with each other. The dialogue proceeds in short bursts, interrupted monologues punctuated by brief silences which, Friel indicates, '*occur like regular cadences*'. He adds, '*To defeat them someone always introduces a fresh theme*' (p. 59).

However, the boys bring an extraordinary energy onto the stage. The dynamic of their rowdy entrance is in sharp contrast to the portrayal of exhaustion at the end of the preceding sequence – only a short silence separates them (pp. 54–5). Friel emphasises their exaggerated laughter, their posing and, above all, their restlessness – '*Tranquility is their enemy: they fight it valiantly*' – and even the game of football is anticipated as a grand excuse for a brawl. The tall tales of their exploits with young women have a similar brutal animation and Private is probably right when he savagely denounces them as 'ignorant bloody louts' (p. 66). The bombast, swagger and sham stories are unconvincing. But we might ask, nevertheless, whether their crudity about sex is a reaction against the teachings of the Church – elsewhere, Private even suggests that they are all still virgins (p. 31). What has the community got to offer these young men, what are their prospects? Jimmy Crerand has emigrated, as have count-less others before him. There is a huge wasted potential here. What could these young men achieve if their aggres-sion and excess energy were channelled into something more purposeful and creative?

The boys are not without some redeeming features. Ned is generous in his gift of the totally inappropriate belt, about which Gar is obviously moved – note that Ned has problems with his father, too (p. 64) – and Joe clearly has a more thoughtful side. Moreover, Private emphasises that 'there *was* fun'. His monologue is another good example of how the tone can change within a speech, moving from a damning condemnation of his friends to a lyrical reconcilation. He recognises his own shortcomings through observing their behaviour – before, he was in-volved in the fooling, but this evening he stands outside the group, looking in. As he thinks of Ballybeg and sees himself 'wanting to hold on to the night', he warms towards them, remembering the 'silly fun and foolish, silly laughing', distilling the images until they are preserved like 'precious gold ...' (p. 66).

THE CANON

Friel's description of the Canon mentions only four things: his lean build, the pallor of his skin and the particular qualities of his eyes and mouth, 'alert' and 'thin' respectively. But it is all you need to know to be able to envisage the whole man and hear his unctuous tones. Canon Mick O'Bryne would naturally be a friend of O'Donnell's – same age, same views and so on – and their evening ritual of draughts and supper provides Private with another opportunity to exercise his satirical wit. But the Canon's function in the play goes beyond the personal. Canon O'Bryne is an establishment figure, a representative of the Catholic Church and as such is responsible for the spiritual life of the community. Again Private, with his face thrust between the Canon and O'Donnell as they play – think about the power of this image – moves from sardonic humour to '*deadly*' seriousness. Private's indictment of the Canon is eloquent; as a priest he should be 'all things to all men' with the ability to explain why we must suffer and how we should endure. But the Canon, who is 'arid', remains silent, too circumspect to speak. Private's tirade concludes: 'Prudence be damned! Christianity isn't prudent – it's insane!' (p. 82). In Gareth's eyes the failure of the Church to 'translate all this loneliness, this groping, this dreadful bloody buffoonery' into something meaningful which 'will make life bearable for us all', is total.

Friel skilfully manipulates all the various elements of this scene and it is worth taking the time to imagine how it plays on stage (pp. 76–85). The sustained visual image of the two men bent over their game of draughts is played simultaneously with, and set against, three main phases of action which vary in pace, rhythm and tone accordingly: O'Donnell and the Canon's measured movement and clichéd conversation counterpointed by Private's barbed comments, followed briefly by Madge and Public's aside conducted in undertones; Private's fierce confrontations with O'Donnell and the Canon, the juxtaposition of his syncopated pop song with the haunting melody of 'Auld Lang Syne' segueing into the Mendelssohn, the sound of which fills the stage; and the final sequence between O'Donnell and the Canon with the muted strains of the violin concerto in the background. Friel indicates a slow curtain so the visual image and the sound of the violin both linger. Look also for tiny but telling details, such as the unexpected sound of O'Donnell's 'short dry laugh', which all add to the texture of the scene.

KATE (KATIE, KATHY) DOOGAN/MRS KING

Gar uses all three diminutives of Kate Doogan's name, Kathy being the most intimate. Look to see when and in what form he speaks her name, as it will give you a clue to his emotional state. The Irish have embodied the romantic ideal of Ireland in 'Kathleen ni Houlihan', so Kate's full name has a particular resonance. Appropriately, she is associated in Gar's mind with traditional Irish music, his first recollection of her in the play prompted by the ceilidh music – 'Katie's tune'. Gareth loved her once, 'wanted so much to marry her that it was a bloody sickness'. Private calls Public 'randy boy' and asks insistently, 'Do you still love her? Do you still lust after her?' (p. 14). The two sides of Gar's person have different views of Kate: Public recalls her as 'sweet Katie Doogan ... my darling Kathy Doogan ...', while Private remembers her as an 'Aul bitch ... Rotten aul snobby bitch!' Public blames himself for losing her, Private sees only the betrayal. During the first part of the scene between Public and Kate, Private appears to remain in the present, watching the couple and occasionally mimicking Kate's middle-class tones. Thus we see Public in the foreground madly in love and in lust with Kate. She appears to reciprocate his feelings but is very clear-eyed about what will impress her father. Her rapid instructions to Public – 'You have £20 a week and £5,000 in the bank and your father's about to retire' (p. 18) – are perceptive advice. Friel gives no physical description of Kate whatsoever but she is obviously attractive and, unfortunately for Gar, literally out of his class.

49

Losing Kathy, and under such humiliating circumstances, was 'a sore hoke on the aul prestige' and has left
'a deep scar on the aul skitter of a soul' (p. 22). Gar cut a
diffident and obsequious figure in his interview with
Doogan and his economic insecurity was no basis for a
marriage to a young woman who lives at 'Gortmore
House'. Despite the Senator's assurances, spoken *with
sincerity*, that any decision Kate makes in choosing a
husband will be her own, she bends predictably to her
father's wishes. Part of Gar cannot forget the betrayal
but part of him yearns for her. Public calls her name at
the end of Episode One as he struggles to reassert his
enthusiasm for Philadelphia (p. 36); she is clearly on his
mind a short time later at the beginning of Episode Two
as Public sings the folk song (p. 37); on re-reading Aunt
Lizzy's letter, Public recites the words of Kathy's wedding
invitation (p. 43); and she is in the background of Gar's
thoughts throughout the scene with the Americans
(pp. 43–51). Thus Friel brings Kate into focus several
times between her two appearances, reminding us of the
depth of Gar's pain.

Gar is completely taken by surprise, however, when
Kate calls to say goodbye. She and Public sit and exchange
pleasantries, during which Kate introduces the notion of
Gar's emigration yielding material success: 'You'll do
well, Gar; make a lot of money, and come back here in
twenty years' time, and buy the whole village.' Unable to
cope with Kate's response to his enquiry after Dr King,
Public takes his cue from this earlier remark and launches
into a vain boast about making his first million (p. 68).
Fuelled by Kate's presence, something in Public snaps. All
his frustration and the emotional turmoil caused by the
failure of his relationships with his father and Kate, are

suddenly projected onto his hatred for Ballybeg. He aggressively denounces his birthplace, taunting Kate for staying. But this does not come from the heart and he resorts to quoting Master Boyle: 'Impermanence – anonymity – that's what I'm looking for; a vast restless place that doesn't give a damn about the past' (p. 69).

Kate makes an excuse to leave – this is not the Gar she remembers. Unfortunately, she chooses to use Francis King as her reason for leaving which elicits a reckless response from Public (p. 70). His goodbye to Kate is inadequate, a platitude echoing Ned's farewell to him – 'And if you can't be good – you know?' – which denies the tenderness of their past friendship. It is interesting that in the scene with Kate, Private has no influence over Public, suggesting that neither side of the man is in control. After Kate has gone Gar appears to be in the grip of a breakdown. Look carefully at Public's actions and his attempts to whistle 'Philadelphia' and see how Private's incessant talking, usually so elegantly shaped, is composed of snatches of previous conversations, creating a montage of incoherence (pp. 70–71). He is left with Kate's words echoing in his ears as Public calls upon his father to 'say something!' (p. 71).

THE SWEENEYS AND BEN BURTON

I have left the Sweeneys till last for you to consider exactly what it is that Gareth is being offered in America. Friel sets the scene in some detail and gives useful information about Con's manner and Lizzy's appearance (p. 43). Lizzy is very tactile and Friel points out that this *constant physical touching is new and disquieting to Public*. She also moves around the kitchen as she speaks and you should examine the scene with this in mind; it is not completely static as might be suggested from the page. Friel is careful to mention that no one is drunk but the scene does have a considerable emotional charge which informs Gar and Lizzy's responses – she is coping with returning to her homeland, he is sitting out Kathy's wedding to which his father has gone. Aunt Lizzy talks about their good friends, emphasising Ben's generosity towards them; Americans have a 'can-do' philosophy exemplified by Con's success from humble beginnings; and their numerous possessions and considerable assets confirm the affluence and opportunity that America offers (pp. 49–50). We know already from Lizzy's letter that Gar will have his own room with air-conditioning, TV, and ensuite bathroom. He also has a job (pp. 41–2).

Private is initially terrified when he realises that Gar's presence in America would complete the Sweeneys' family life but, swayed by his own and Lizzy's desolation, Public impetuously makes his fateful decision. Con's note of caution is ignored as Public opens himself to the possibility of a surrogate love. Private briefly recoils from the thought of Lizzy's touch but as Public is embraced by Lizzy, Private ends the scene in a state of '*happy anguish*' (p. 51). In the time that has elasped since the Sweeneys' visit, Gar has not really resolved these conflicting emotions, as evidenced by Private and Public's exchange when the flashback dissolves (pp. 52–3).

One final point: why is Ben Burton in the scene? He is a quiet American, polite and discreet, rather different from some of the cartoon types that people Gar's fantasies. Moreover he is an Episcopalian who Private refers to as a 'right sort' and 'a right skin' (pp. 42–3). Please note, however, Father O'Flaherty's view of those who are not of the Roman Catholic faith (pp. 48–9). Ben says very little but Lizzy draws him into the conversation when she wants confirmation that 'America's Gawd's own country,' and his opinion as to whether Gar should emigrate. His response is equivocal: 'It's just another place to live, Elise. Ireland – America – what's the difference?' (p. 49).

Endnote

Paradoxically for a play about non-communication and failure, *Philadelphia* is a remarkably accessible and energising experience in the theatre. Its humour and wit provoke much laughter but the comedy is inevitably tinged throughout by grief. The main conduit of the play's emotional current is, of course, the divided character of Gareth O'Donnell. This device is not only a theatrical tour de force in its depiction of a wide range of emotion, from histrionics through violent rage to extreme tenderness, but also offers an intellectual challenge to the audience as Gar struggles to understand his condition of alienation. In a way it is a rite of passage as Gar is forced to accept the responsibilities of manhood in a world which he perceives as godless and cruel.

Friel leaves the ending open. Nothing is resolved. Throughout the play Gareth has spent more time contemplating the past than the future and his enthusiasm for America has significantly diminished the nearer it gets to the time for his departure. He is painfully aware of the paucity of life in Ballybeg but he is equally mindful of the vulgar materialism of American city life. He will not escape family ties by going to Philadelphia – will Aunt Lizzy's suffocating love be any easier to bear than his father's cold indifference? We know that Gareth's problem lies at a deeper level. The two most important relationships of his life have failed. He wooed Kate, but his socio-economic status was not sufficient to win her. Denied a mother, he can only look to his father for a full expression of parental love. Gar remembers that once upon a time he shared moments of happiness and joy with his father. O'Donnell too can remember such feelings, but because he never reveals this to Gar the state of non-communication between them continues. Both men are trapped, each with an emotional tie to the other but incapable of expressing their love. Perhaps Madge's bleak conclusion is the right one. Gar will inherit his father's legacy and turn out just like him, having learnt nothing on the way.

Textual Notes

ix O'Donnell – the O'Donnells were one of the eminent families of Gaelic Ireland based in Donegal.

xi *scullery* – a small room where dishes are washed up and rough household work is done. This denotes the age of the building.

xii *Ceilidh music* – traditional Gaelic Irish music.

– '*All Round My Hat*' – a traditional song.

– '*She Moved through the Fair*' – a haunting folk song.

– '*California, Here I Come!*' – popular American song.

– '*Give the Woman in the Bed more Porter*' – a music-hall song.

2 pokes – small sack; 'buying a pig in a poke' – i.e., without seeing the goods.

3 Angelus – a Roman Catholic prayer to commemorate the Incarnation said in the early morning, at noon and at sunset, when a bell is rung.

- bugger – so-and-so; a colloquial term of abuse, not strong.
6 eejit[ing] – idiot.
- aul duck – term of endearment.
7 Skinflint – miser.
- Skittery – silly.
8 yarning – talking.
- Nicodemus – the devil.
- bagatelle – an unimportant trifle.
9 St Patrick's Pilgrimage – see note below on Lough Derg, p. 23.
10 St Harold's Cross – an area of Dublin.
11 side-car – passenger attachment for a motor-cycle.
- Bundoran – one of the most popular seaside resorts in Ireland.
13 *lilts* – vocal accompaniment to traditional dance.
15 get – bastard.
18 Senator Doogan – is a member of the Senate, the upper house of the Irish parliament. Senators are nominated by the Taoiseach (prime minister) or elected by university graduates and councillors from around the country.
22 Sligo – the main town in County Sligo.
- Malahide – a small town on the coast not far from Dublin.
- Knights – Knights of St Columbanus, a secret Catholic organisation which promotes anti-liberal views.
- Masons – Freemasonry is a secret organisation, banned by the Catholic Church, which confers definite business and social advantages – particularly in small communities where the leading middle-class figures are members.

23 Lough Derg – in the middle of the lough is Station Island, which serves as a retreat for Catholics in need of rigour and solitude to recharge their faith; hence the reference to 'bare feet'. St Patrick is believed to have stayed and fasted.

26 Marie Celeste – a ghost ship. No one on board.

31 the length of – as far as.

 – Strabane – a border town on the eastern edge of County Donegal.

33 the digs – his lodgings; Boyle is not a man of property.

34 ten shillings – 50p; pre-decimilisation when Ireland still used old sterling currency.

40 fluke – something very small or nothing at all.

42 Belmullet – a town founded in 1825 in one of the most isolated areas of Ireland.

57 take a running race – have some sense.

58 crack – fun, gossip.

59 skivvies – maids of all work.

60 in the pelt – naked.

62 a bob – one shilling (5p).

64 scut – a contemptible person.

 – aul fella – Ned's father.

65 taking a hand – making fun; joshing.

72 *rosary* – a set of prayers.

 – *decade* – division of the rosary comprising ten Ave Marias, one Pater Noster and one Gloria Patri.

82 Gregorian – as in a ritual Gregorian chant.

88 plug tobacco – a cake of tobacco.

Translations

The Play

Translations is set in 1833 in a hedge-school in Baile Beag/
Ballybeg, an Irish-speaking community in County
Donegal. The British Army are making the first Ordnance
Survey map of Ireland, Anglicising all the Irish names en
route, and the new National Schools are being established
to impose English as the national language. The play is
about language and, in particular, the death of the Irish
language and the implicit loss of cultural and national
identity. The theme is personalised through the experience
of the people of Baile Beag and in particular the
O'Donnell family: Hugh, father and schoolmaster;
Manus, eldest son and scholar; and Owen, the 'exiled'
younger son who returns as a 'translator' for the British
Army. These are turbulent times for the community,
which also lives with the recurring threat of the potato
blight, and under the shadow of eviction and emigration.
The historical moment at which the play is set will bring
irreversible change for Baile Beag and its people and, by
extension, the whole of Ireland.

Friel's primary sources were accounts of the Ordnance
Survey by Colonel Thomas Colby, John Andrews and
John O'Donovan; *The Hedge-Schools of Ireland* by P. J.
Dowling; and George Steiner's *After Babel*. He also went
to Urris in the Inishowen Peninsula – his setting for this
Ballybeg – where he felt 'some sense of how the ordinary

British sappers might have reacted to this remote, bleak, desolate strip of land attenuated between mountain and sea'. ('Extracts from a Sporadic Diary', Tim Pat Coogan, ed., *Ireland and the Arts*, London: Quartet, n.d., p. 59). Friel maintains that the cultural climate of Baile Beag 'is a dying climate – no longer quickened by its past, about to be plunged almost overnight into an alien future' (Sporadic Diary, p. 59). Baile Beag, despite its seductive beauty, is no idyll or Arcadia. Yolland, from the position of an outsider, finds a community 'at its ease and with its own conviction and assurance' (p. 48), but Friel claims 'this is a complete illusion, since you have on stage the representatives of a certain community – one is dumb, one is lame and one is alcoholic, a physical maiming which is a public representation of their spiritual deprivation' ('Talking to ourselves', Brian Friel talks to Paddy Agnew, *Magill*, December 1980, p. 61).

The community's material deprivation is compensated for by the opulence and ostentation of its language, which is 'full of mythologies of fantasy, hope and self-deception' (p. 42). For the British, language is power, for the Irish it is a form of romantic evasion, their 'only method of replying to ... inevitabilities'. Friel's concern is to maintain a balance between the '*public* concern of the theme: how does the eradication of the Irish language and the substitution of English affect this particular *society*?' and 'the exploration of the dark and private places of individual souls' (Sporadic Diary, p. 60). Friel achieves a fine tension between the individual and the society, and between the two worlds of the colonial and the colonised. He also gives us a remarkable love story where these worlds collide, as Maire and Yolland dare to cross the tribal divide with terrible consequences.

Yolland's abduction by the Donnelly twins precipitates retaliatory measures by the British Army that are swift and violent. Owen's homecoming is complete when he recognises that he has betrayed his ancestral roots. Towards the end of the play, in the midst of the chaos and incoherence, Hugh toasts Jimmy: 'My friend, confusion is not an ignoble condition.' Friel, who confesses to living in confusion himself, believes that 'Hugh's words are perhaps a fairly accurate description of how we all live, specifically at the present time. Other countries perhaps have access to more certainties than we have at the moment. I was talking specifically about Ireland' (*Magill*, p. 61).

In order to portray an Irish-speaking community, Friel devises a 'theatrical conceit' by which 'even though the actors speak English – the audience will assume or accept that they are speaking Irish' (Sporadic Diary, p. 57). This is the play's major formal innovation. Irony is the chief dramatic method which runs throughout the play, reinforced by its historical setting. The greatest irony of all, however, is that all the Irish characters are obliged to speak in English to be understood by an audience, including an Irish one.

Historical Context

It is helpful to consider *Translations* from three historical perspectives: events in the past which profoundly affected the relationship between Ireland and Britain and of which the characters in the play would be aware; developments in Ireland during the period in which the play is set that will bring about irrevocable changes in the lives of the Irish people; and with the wisdom of hindsight, which would inform a contemporary audience's response to the ideas explored in the play.

Past

One major date is referred to in the play – the Rebellion of 1798 which Hugh and Jimmy set out to join. This was launched in the May of that year by the United Irishmen, a society formed by Wolfe Tone, a Protestant barrister, in Belfast in 1791. Inspired by the French Revolution, its aims were to unite Protestants and Catholics behind a revolutionary programme to radicalise the Irish Parliament in Dublin, and to remove British rule from Ireland. Despite French assistance, the rising was a disaster in political terms, the rebels enjoying success only in parts of County Antrim, County Down and County Wexford. Here they held out for several weeks until the Government built up an overwhelming force against the rebels, who were finally defeated in June at the Battle of Vinegar Hill. Another French fleet arrived in August, too late. The French–Irish Army failed to provoke the broad popular rising it expected and the rebellion was crushed with unprecedented ferocity, hangings, burnings and floggings being common punishments. Wolfe Tone was captured but committed suicide in prison before the British could execute him. The insurrections organised by the United Irishmen persuaded Pitt, the British Prime Minister, to carry through the Act of Union in 1800. But despite the concessions received under the new law, the scar of the repression of the 1798 Rising was set deep in Irish folk memory.

In addition to Hugh's personal recollection of the uprising, Doalty refers to reprisals meted out by the British in his grandfather's lifetime. Certainly there are precedents for Lancey's action.

Present

A general survey of Ireland was advocated by the Spring Rice Report to the British Government in 1824. The survey was seen as a 'civil measure' but acknowledged that it was 'not unimportant in a military point of view'. The final sentence of the report is echoed in Lancey's words when he addresses Hugh and the hedge-school pupils in Act One: 'In that portion of the Empire to which it more particularly applies, it cannot but be received as a proof of the disposition of the legislature to adopt all measures calculated to advance the interests of Ireland.' The Ordnance Survey of Ireland involved not only mapping the whole island but also renaming every place in the country. This was a mammoth task carried out by specially trained officers and men from the Corps of Royal Engineers. Ireland was, and is still, rich in place names, the vast majority of which describe natural features – a great lexicon of the language, a series of definitions. Unfortunately, in many cases, a feature that was all too evident when the name was first given may have changed out of all recognition – the lake dried up, the site built upon, the monument destroyed and so on. This is the problem Owen and Yolland have with Tobair Vree where the original meaning has been 'eroded'.

The National Schools were introduced to Ireland from 1831 and, as Bridget correctly reports, they were free and all instruction was given in English. Thus a state system of education was established, a measure hastened by a British Government alarmed by the continuing vigour of the hedge-schools, which tended to engender nationalistic convictions in rural districts. J. P. Dowling considered hedge-schools to be the most 'vital force in popular education in Ireland in the eighteenth century'. He explains further:

[they] owed their origin to the suppression of all ordinary legitimate means of education, first during the Cromwellian regime and then under the Penal Code introduced in the reign of William III and operating from that time till within less than twenty years from the opening of the nineteenth century ... [they] were clearly of peasant institution ... maintained by the people who wanted their children educated; and they were taught by men who came from the people. (Dowling, 1935, reprinted in the programme of Field Day's première production)

Even the humblest of the schools gave basic instruction in reading, writing and arithmetic. In a great number of schools, Latin, Greek, mathematics and other subjects were also taught. In most cases the work was done entirely through the medium of the Irish language.

The National Schools were a threat to this indigenous form of learning, the Irish language and the old Gaelic traditions. But the Irish language was already in decline. Tom Paulin confirms that 'English was the language of power, commerce and social acceptance, and the Irish people largely accepted Daniel O'Connell's view that Gaelic monolingualism was an obstacle to freedom' ('A New Look at the Language Question', *Ireland's Field Day*, London: Hutchinson, 1985, p. 10). You will remember that Maire also cites Daniel O'Connell (1775–1847), who worked ceaselessly for Catholic emancipation. Hugh dismisses English as a language only fit for commerce, but he is missing, or deliberately ignoring, the point that O'Connell was to make so forcibly at his massive gatherings across the country.

In addition to these two major initiatives introduced by

the British in the 1830s, the threat of the potato blight, the reality of evictions and the possibility of emigration are ever present in the background to the daily lives of the people of Ballybeg.

Hindsight

The terrible Famine of 1845 and the subsequent massive emigration of Irish citizens to the USA, Canada, Britain, Australia and New Zealand, are foreshadowed by references in the text to potato blight, Maire's passage money and relatives in the New World. The fraught history of Ireland during most of the nineteenth and twentieth centuries is, of course, not mentioned, but we should assume that it is so deeply rooted in Irish consciousness as to provide part of the context of the play.

In the decade that preceded the première of the play, internment without trial was introduced; the event known as Bloody Sunday occurred in Derry; the Sunningdale Agreement failed following Protestant strikes and UDA atrocities; the retaliatory IRA bombed Birmingham; the Prevention of Terrorism Act, allowing delayed detention without charge, was introduced; the Blanket Protest took place, and Britain was found guilty of 'inhuman and degrading' treatment of prisoners by the European Court of Human Rights. In 1980 the hunger strikes began in Belfast. Thus Friel conceived and wrote the play towards the end of the most turbulent period of Irish history since Partition.

The Stage-World

Locale

Baile Beag is placed in the context of a wider world. We hear of Nova Scotia, Boston and Brooklyn, places where the people of the townland have relatives or, as in Maire's case, aspire to emigrate. They are in touch with these places through letters, gifts which they receive (e.g., Sarah's dress, p. 78) and the promise of passage money. We are also made aware of the whole island of Ireland: Dublin, Omagh, Ennis, Kerry and Mayo are all mentioned. The physical features of Baile Beag and the Donegal landscape are described by Friel in some detail – bogland, turf-banks, hay fields, salmon streams, cliffs, gaps and so on.

There are a number of families and individuals living in the community, some of whom do not appear in the play but have a significant effect upon the lives of those who do – for example, Maire's siblings, Anna na mBreag, Con Connie Tim, Nellie Ruadh, Bridget's brother Seamus, the Donnelly twins, and Mr George Alexander, the local Justice of the Peace. The English name is relevant here, reflecting the imposed authority of a British judicial system. There are references as well to a cultural life – the various classes at the hedge-school, the dances when the Fiddler O'Shea is about, the musical evenings at Maire's house – and some evidence of religious activity in the community. The parish priest lives at Lis na Muc – Hugh dismisses him as barely literate, which may or may not be true – and he presumably conducts the christening and funeral of Nellie Ruadh's baby, but there is little emphasis on a Catholic way of life.

As in *Philadelphia*, the central family in the play are the O'Donnells. This time the father is named Hugh, thus, ironically, sharing his name with Red Hugh O'Donnell of Tyrconnell (now Donegal) a hero of the great sagas. But our Hugh shows no such heroic tendencies, preferring the quiet life of a poet and schoolmaster. Both his sons are cultured men fluent in Greek, Latin and English, but are contrasted physically, temperamentally and politically. It is important, however, to remember that there is no mother. She is mentioned only at the end of the play by Hugh, who calls her his 'goddess' – black-haired Caitlin, daughter of Reactainn – but Friel makes it clear that the O'Donnell home is *'comfortless and dusty and functional'* with *'no trace of a woman's hand'* (p. 1).

Setting

Friel gives a detailed description of the barn. The lower part, which we see, is a public area where the school is held, the upper part, which is offstage, is a private area where the O'Donnells live. The barn is full of *'broken and forgotten implements'* and is itself *'disused'* and dusty (p. 1). The room is *'functional'*, the furniture is rudimentary, and the towel draped over the pail of water at the door is soiled. We see an old world in a state of neglect and decay, the people within it struggling to make a living and sustain a culture against all the odds. The crude, rural setting is important to achieve as it needs to offset the beauty of the environs as described in the text. The picturesque should be avoided at all costs – remember Jimmy wears filthy clothes, and Hugh and Manus are shabbily dressed. Owen and the soldiers are outsiders in this world – well dressed and well fed.

Friel places each scene at a specific time of day, which

has implications for lighting and sound. The late summer afternoon and evening ambience adds to the romance of the story before and during the dance. The scene which follows as the rain lashes and the storm clouds gather is in stark contrast. The mood and atmosphere of the various scenes would be suitably supported by the subtle use of lighting and 'natural' sound. Friel indicates music at the end of Act Two, Scene One, to aid the climactic moment and propel the action into the following scene. Music of the appropriate tone, quality and rhythm could be used at the beginning and end of each scene at a director's discretion without detracting from the playwright's intention.

Dramatic Structure

Translations has a conventional three-act structure: Act One introduces all the characters and sets up the situation with some exposition; Act Two, Scene One, explores and develops the argument of the play; Act Two, Scene Two, depicts an act of transgression; Act Three shows the effect of this action. There is no resolution – the ending is open and ambiguous. The linear development of the play's action is contained within this structure which is framed by the birth and death of Nellie Ruadh's baby. But Friel employs other structural devices which interface with this basic framework and which are themselves also thematic. We have already established that the play is about language and explores notions of naming and translation. These ideas are brought in and out of focus across the pattern of action, interacting and commenting upon each other.

We will now look at how language in its various

manifestations is presented in the play and then consider the significance and presentation of naming and translation.

Language

Friel solves the problem of the English/Irish language convention with apparent ease. We are reminded many times that the Irish characters are speaking Gaelic: for example, Maire tells Jimmy that she only has three words of English (p. 8); Lancey asks Owen/Roland if the hedge-school pupils speak '*any* English' (p. 32); Owen asks Manus to speak in English in the presence of Yolland (p. 42); and Maire and Yolland have great difficulty in communicating with each other (pp. 59–61). There are the passages of translation which Owen effects between Lancey and the community, and between Yolland and Maire. The Irish characters are distinguished by their speech idiom, Hiberno-English, which is evident to a greater or lesser degree depending on their education. Jimmy, despite his knowledge of Greek and Latin, is probably the most extreme example, designating him also as the character with lowest social status. And when the play is in performance the Irish characters are clearly defined by their accents. Friel writes in his 'Sporadic Diary' that he was concerned 'to create each voice and endow it with its appropriate pitch' (p. 59), and each voice, be it Irish or English, has its own characteristic speech-patterns and idiosyncrasies of expression.

We are introduced also to Greek and Latin – Hugh, Manus, Owen and Jimmy Jack are fluent in both languages. Friel always gives a translation in the body of the text as part of the dialogue – Hugh's linguistic game with the class is particularly effective here. Hugh writes poetry in Latin and Jimmy lives between the covers of Homer's works. Through the languages they all keep in touch with these ancient civilisations, their philosophies and their literature, and the collective wisdom derived from them. To Hugh, Jimmy and Manus these languages are not dead, they are very much part of their daily lives, but knowledge of them will not equip these scholars to deal with the changing reality of the world in which they live. Their own language of Irish is to them also a living thing, but to the outside world it is effectively dead or dying. Owen knows this and so too does Hugh, who says: 'But remember that words are signals, counters. They are not immortal. And it can happen ... that a civilisation can be imprisoned in a linguistic contour which no longer matches the landscape of ... fact' (p. 52).

Metaphorically, language is the means by which the British Army rapes the land, one culture penetrating the other. Owen creates a litany of Irish place-names which Yolland uses to woo Maire. Towards the end of the play Lancey inverts the litany, ordering Owen to translate from English into Irish so that the locals will know which of their townlands are under threat of extinction (pp. 79–80). These place-names take on symbolic significance as the events of the play unfold, as does the character of Sarah, the mute girl initially without language at all. Through Manus's careful teaching she learns to speak, but when confronted by Lancey she is unable to articulate the words, eventually retreating back into silence (p. 83). Seamus Heaney interprets this moment 'as if some symbolic figure of Ireland from an eighteenth-century vision poem, the one who once confidently called herself Cathleen Ni Houlihan, has been struck dumb by the shock of modernity' ('Stories of Imperialism ... English and Irish', *Times Literary Supplement*, 24 October 1980, p. 1199).

The establishment of English as the first language in Ireland is seen as inevitable and by many as a good thing. However, Maire wishes to learn English in order to emigrate to America, not to improve her generation's situation for her own and Ireland's benefit as O'Connell advocated. Manus, who in some ways is the guardian of the language, sees this as a double betrayal against himself and their homeland. But in the event, Manus is incapable of defending that which he holds sacred. As he admits, before his voluntary exile, he made 'The wrong gesture in the wrong language' (p. 70).

Naming

In his 'Sporadic Diary', Friel writes that he was 'reluctant even to name the characters, maybe because the naming-taming process is what the play is about' (p. 58). All the Irish characters are referred to by their Christian names, suggesting a degree of familiarity, whereas the English are referred to by their surnames – only Owen and Maire call Yolland George – thus distancing them somewhat from the audience. Lancey does not have a Christian name, distancing him even further. Maire, Manus, Doalty, Bridget, Hugh and Owen are all well-known Irish names, with the latter two also common in Wales. Sarah, James and John (for Jimmy Jack) are universal names. Lancey has connotations of the military and sounds English, whereas Yolland is a blend of 'Old' and 'land'. 'Yola' was also the name given to the form of English spoken by the first English-speaking settlers in Ireland. They eventually gave up their own language and adopted the language and customs of the indigenous Irish.

Thus Yolland, given his origins and aspirations, is appropriately named.

Name and identity are synonymous throughout the play – Sarah's first words are an act of personal identification; Owen eventually insists that his name is not Roland and begins to reclaim his Irish self. The play starts with a christening which Hugh calls the 'ritual of naming' (p. 21), and Owen and Yolland effect 'A hundred christenings! A thousand baptisms!' as they 'name a thing and – bang – it leaps into existence!' (pp. 55–6). When Sarah is unable to speak her name at the end of the play she essentially loses her personal identity. This effectively is what happens to Ireland in national terms as, inexorably and irrevocably, the country, in its minutest detail, is renamed.

Translation

Friel makes it clear that there are different forms of translation in the play, hence the plural title *Translations*. The most obvious is the translation from one language into another. The cover of the Faber playtext is again instructive. It shows a signpost with the Gaelic name (Dun Na Gall in Irish script) above and the English 'equivalent' (Donegal) below. Donegal's original name was *Tir Chonaill*, which translates as 'the land of Conal'. In the early seventeenth century, the English changed the name to that of their main garrison, *Dun na nGall* – 'the fort of the foreigner'. The play is set in a Gaelic-speaking area and yet its Irish name denotes that foreigners had already settled there, the place-name changed accordingly. But with the arrival of more foreigners in the shape of Lancey and Yolland the name is now to be translated, Anglicised.

Perhaps we should pause to consider at this point whether it is possible to translate satisfactorily from one language to another. The evidence of thousands of translations of texts on every conceivable subject would suggest that it is. However, can meaning be conveyed accurately, is there always a perfect equivalent available? The example that Friel gives when Owen is trying to determine the translation of 'Bun na hAbhann' is interesting: 'Bun is the Irish word for bottom. And Abha means river. So it's literally the mouth of the river' (p. 39). 'River' translates directly but 'bottom' and 'mouth' are two completely different things. Owen finally settles on 'Burnfoot' which is a kind of poetic approximation, thus effecting a further translation.

Yolland, who longs to speak Irish, suspects that he can never become one of the tribe: 'Even if I did speak Irish I'd always be an outsider here, wouldn't I? I may learn the password but the language of the tribe will always elude me, won't it? The private core will always be ... hermetic, won't it?' Owen assures him that 'You can learn to decode us' (p. 48). Hugh returns to the subject in Act Three, prompted by Maire's request to learn English: 'We'll begin tomorrow ... But don't expect too much. I will provide you with the available words and the available grammar. But will that help you to interpret between privacies? I have no idea. But it's all we have. I have no idea at all' (pp. 89–90). What the audience has witnessed in the interim is the scene between Maire and Yolland when the lovers appear to communicate for a short time on an inspirational level. As soon as language comes between them they struggle to understand each other. The litany of place-names, which in this context essentially has no specific meaning but touches at the heart of Maire's being, mysteriously brings them together, only for the audience to discover when they speak in their respective languages that their desire for one another is based on entirely different premises – Yolland wants to stay with Maire in Baile Beag, a place where he feels he can 'live'; Maire sees Yolland as a way of escaping from her homeland to a better life elsewhere. The scene starts by suggesting that communication between the two worlds, the two cultures, is possible, but because, ironically, the two individuals think and perceive things differently, that promise is never fulfilled.

Other forms and examples of translation in the play relate to the interpretation of facts, historical or otherwise: Owen's misrepresentation of Lancey in Act One; the naming of Tobair Vree in Act Two; Owen's reinvention of himself as Roland; Maire and Yolland's attempt to transform their lives through their mutual love; and Jimmy Jack's removal from an earthly state to a completely imagined life; and so on.

The Stage-Action

I have provided a commentary on the stage-action to show how the themes of language and translation are dramatised, and at the same time to determine what motivates the characters in relation to the changing situation. This last is more complex than it might at first appear, largely because Friel deals in ambiguity. It is also helpful to imagine how the play might be staged – Act One in particular involves a series of arrivals until the stage is inhabited by ten characters, all of whom have different intentions, responses and rhythms. Friel's stage-craft with regard to exits, entrances and manipulation of the stage-action should all be taken into account when analysing the text.

Act One

Manus, Sarah and Jimmy Jack are discovered as the scene is revealed. Two focal points are established and juxtaposed. Manus is teaching Sarah to speak, while Jimmy Jack sits apart reading quietly aloud in Greek from Homer's *Odyssey*; all three are totally absorbed in their several tasks. Sarah is stubbornly resisting Manus's efforts to get her to speak her name. He is equally insistent, inspired and energised by his mission. His gentle coaxing at the beginning gains her confidence and his instruction to get her tongue and lips working elicits a gradual response. Manus encourages Sarah by telling her to shout out, to release the sound that is pent up inside her, and slowly, painfully, but at the end with a triumphant rush, Sarah gives birth to speech. Manus has been careful to protect her during this delicate time, confiding that what she is trying to do is a secret between them and admonishing Jimmy Jack for interrupting with his audible murmuring. When Sarah finally speaks Manus spontaneously hugs her, much to her '*embarrassed pleasure*', and this intimate moment is capped by Manus's joyous assertion that her achievement heralds a new beginning. Through language, and Manus's care and understanding, Sarah will be able to communicate her previously private thoughts.

Sarah and Manus are living in an intense present with the possibilities of a new future. Meanwhile, Jimmy is living as intensely through the recreation in his imagination of Odysseus/Ulysses's journey in the past. In his translation of the *Odyssey* we see that he revels in the meeting of Odysseus/Ulysses and Athene, comparing himself with the Greek hero in the guise of an old tramp, and extolling the goddess's beauty, remarking with relish on her sexual insatiability. He likens her to an Irish 'goddess', Grania, who also 'can't get her fill of men'. Jimmy's familiarity with these myths, and the immortals and mortals who inhabit them, is apparent. To him, Greece and Baile Beag are synonymous – he refers to Athens as a parish – and sees himself, in his own private fiction, as a potential suitor to Athene.

In this opening sequence the theme of language and the importance of naming are immediately introduced. Sarah literally experiences language for the first time by, significantly, identifying herself. Jimmy is fluent in Greek, moving easily from one language to the other. Manus is even more knowledgeable, assisting Jimmy with his translation. Irony, the chief dramatic method of the play, is also established from the start in Manus's affirmative cry: 'Nothing'll stop us now!' During Jimmy's translation Manus goes upstairs to his living quarters to collect a bowl of milk and some bread. Thus the public and private areas are defined. This extended action also reveals Manus's lameness, and we have time to absorb the poverty of the people, reflected in Manus's shabby clothes and surroundings, Jimmy's filthy garments and Sarah's '*waiflike appearance*'. Her indeterminate age also suggests something timeless and mythical about her.

There is an easy familiarity between the three characters onstage. Manus and Sarah both laugh at Jimmy's '*spasm*' which grips him each time he contemplates Athene's 'flashing eyes'. However, two sequences follow that create a tension in the room. First, Manus is worried and irritated by his father's long absence. At this point we are unaware that Manus is referring to Hugh, but whoever is missing likes to take the drink, as is evident from Sarah's mime. The pub names give more information about the local area and the christening ceremony marks another new beginning. Manus may be secretly pleased that he is obliged to take the class – he has shown himself to be a born teacher and busies himself distributing books, slates, chalk and texts. Sarah chooses this moment to present Manus with a bunch of flowers. Despite her shy manner, Sarah is clearly in love with Manus and might misinterpret his zeal in teaching for another emotion. Unaware of her feelings, he takes the opportunity to encourage a new word from her – 'flowers' – and in return for her effort he kisses the top of her head. This gives rise to the second moment of tension as Manus's innocent act is witnessed and mocked by Maire.

Maire brings with her a can of milk – her payment 'in kind' for tuition at the hedge-school. She takes control of the situation, ignoring Manus, which heightens his unease. Whereas before he was in charge of the territory, Maire's appearance and attitude has reduced his status considerably. Maire joshes playfully with Jimmy Jack, at the same time giving information about the harvest and how hard she is working. The summer is unusually warm and the harvest is the best in living memory. Obviously the sun ripens the hay but the excellent conditions are also favourable for the potato blight which is referred to later. Maire's careless comment, 'I never want to see another like it', is ironic given what transpires. She and Jimmy banter in Latin, thereby introducing another language, and Maire laments her lack of English. It is at this point that we realise all the characters are speaking in Irish.

Maire does not reveal the three English words she knows but speaks a sentence taught to her by her Aunt

Mary. Friel's stage-direction here is important: '(*Her accent is strange because she is speaking a foreign language and because she does not understand what she is saying*)' (p. 8). It is evident that Manus understands the sentence but is ignored by Maire when he corrects her pronunciation of 'maypole'. Jimmy Jack has only one word of English – its meaning consistent with his obsession with the female form. Thus four languages have been introduced arising naturally from the action. Friel's oblique approach enables them to co-exist and comment on each other unobtrusively.

In response to Maire's request for 'a drop of water' – which may also be a ploy to speak to Manus privately – Manus gives her his own bowl of milk. There follows an exchange between the two that tells us a number of important things. The previous evening a social gathering took place at Maire's house which Manus was unable to get to. Instead he spent time writing a letter for Biddy Hanna – indicating the old woman's illiteracy and Manus's generosity – to her sister who has emigrated to Nova Scotia. This is the first reference to a world beyond the immediate community and introduces the ever-present possibility of emigration. Through the gossip we learn of Big Ned Frank (the local stud), Biddy Hanna's opinion of Manus and his father (defined here as a drunk), and the advent of a National School nearby. Maire cannot help laughing at some of this but continues to punish Manus as she dismisses him with the barbed observation, 'Great to be a busy man' (p. 9). It is evident now that a tension exists between the two.

Maire moves away but Manus persistently follows. He heard music coming from Maire's house, a fact confirmed by Maire's remark to Sarah that her father had been 'in great voice'. The evening's revelry, which did not finish until the early hours of the morning, is an example of the cultural life of the community – a counterpoint to the material poverty endured by the locals and manifest onstage. Manus could have joined Maire, but his 'I thought it was too late to call' sounds more like an excuse than an explanation. His offer to help with the harvest the next day is greeted nonchalantly by Maire – the incongruity of 'The Scholar in the Hayfield' being another put down – who tells him that the English sappers are coming to give a hand. The casual introduction of the English military presence into the conversation suggests that the soldiers are by now a familiar sight, and the offer and acceptance of help is a sign that the relationship between them and the local community is, on the surface, harmonious. Neither can understand the other but Maire does not seem to think it matters. Again she will be proved wrong. Whether Manus is just at the end of his tether or mention of the soldiers additionally annoys him, he at last confronts Maire's bad mood.

Bridget and Doalty prevent any further discussion, however. Their boisterous arrival brings a particular energy onstage. The young man and woman are representatives of the ordinary members of the local community and it is through them that we learn much of what goes on outside the hedge-school. Doalty gives his party piece – a rather good imitation of the Master – while Bridget tells us of Hugh's whereabouts. Although Doalty's command of Latin is limited he enjoys playing with language – note his attempt at rhyme. However, Maire is more interested in the pole that Doalty is brandishing. Doalty's account of the Red Coats' activities reveals a further connection between the soldiers and Maire (they leave the theodolite in her byre) and she clearly disapproves of Doalty's pranks. Manus, however, interprets Doalty's 'gesture' as a way of indicating 'a presence'. Whether Doalty's actions are as politically motivated as Manus suggests is not clear. Doalty has definitely stolen the pole and Bridget is convinced that he will be arrested. This focus on his behaviour triggers a characteristic response from Doalty, who rapidly changes the subject as he grabs hold of Bridget (p. 12). But Manus's observation is an important one. It puts him further at odds with Maire but is also an indicator to the audience of Manus's hostility (albeit mildly expressed) to the British presence in the locality.

The class begins. The stage-picture shows the group inhabiting the space, taking up their places, washing hands, combing hair, etc., while Bridget introduces the subject of the christening of Nellie Ruadh's baby. The significance of naming is this time accompanied by ribald comments as to the identity of the baby's father. Doalty deflects the possibility of any personal involvement onto Jimmy, although decides not to pursue the joke too far. Instead he refers to Jimmy's knowledge of Horace, which reminds Jimmy of Virgil's *Georgics*. There follows an interesting passage in which Jimmy argues, with reference to the Latin text, that Doalty is sowing the wrong seeds. Jimmy is right – if more land had been given over to corn instead of potatoes, the blight would not prove so devastating in the years to come. Initially Doalty plays the fool but after Jimmy's admonishments his riposte is more spirited and he hides his true emotion by grabbing Sarah. Manus takes the heat out of the situation by asserting his authority and enquiring as to the where-abouts of the missing members of the class.

The mood in the hedge-school changes. Sean Beag, who

has gone fishing for salmon, presents no problem, but at the mention of the Donnelly twins, *'suddenly the atmosphere is silent and alert'* (p. 15). Doalty is non-committal and will not yield when pressed by Manus. Doalty is playfully subversive in the classroom but it is unlikely that he is involved in local resistance. However, he clearly knows more than he is prepared to tell. Bridget gives the game away by passing on her brother Seamus's news about the soldiers' horses being found at the foot of the cliffs nearby. By association the Donnelly twins are implicated in this act of sabotage. Bridget realises her mistake and attempts to change the subject but interestingly Manus does not pursue his enquiry. Instead he has a word for each of his charges, whispering quietly to Sarah as he makes his way finally to Maire.

The exchange between Maire and Manus reveals the difficulties that beset their relationship. Having not seen each other over the weekend, Maire has been unable to tell him about the arrival of the passage money. Maire is using the threat of emigration as a lever to get Manus to apply for the job at the new National School. Maire's situation at home is dire – she has ten siblings and no father to support the family – and a better future is either marriage to Manus or emigration. £56 a year is a good salary, but despite his promise Manus has not yet applied. Is Manus's reluctance to compete against his father borne of fear or a sense of responsibility? Both are possible. Whenever Maire asks Manus a direct question he responds by asking another or becomes evasive. Maire is convinced that Hugh would not get the job given his age and habitual drinking (this is implied rather than directly stated) but Manus is adamant in his decision not to 'go in against him' (p. 17). Maire's frustration is evident and she quickly breaks the intimacy of their conversation, turning pointedly to Bridget to enquire about her brother Seamus's trip to Port. It is important to note that Sarah has been trying to listen to part of the conversation between Manus and Maire. Probably in the staging the two could be set slightly apart from the rest of the class, thus making Sarah's inquisitiveness more intrusive – Friel indicates that she is '*at his shoulder*' (p. 17).

Bridget mentions in passing that the soldiers are making maps near the gap of Cnoc na Mona, but the main point of her story is Seamus's report of the sweet smell that heralds the beginning of a potato blight. Bridget sees more danger in the sweet smell than the presence of the soldiers, who are becoming a familiar sight in the parish. Maire's outburst lists the predominant fears of the community: the potato blight leading to famine, rent increases, harvest failures on land and sea, and evictions (p. 18). She despairs of the local attitude that looks for disaster. Doalty defuses the row by agreeing with Maire, quoting St Colmcille's 'prophecy', and changes the subject to the new National School. Doalty asks Jimmy if he should apply for the headship, an idea that Maire picks up in order to needle Manus. Bridget goes on to give information, which she has gleaned from brother Seamus, including the fact that every subject will be taught in English. Bridget's reference to the Buncrana people reflects the more advanced education of the town community as opposed to those in rural areas. The discussion about the new school, and the imposition of the English language, denotes that an inevitable and irreversible process is in train. Friel introduces all these major ideas in a very natural and relaxed way through the small talk, swapping of gossip and easy chat of the class.

Sarah's grunt and mime warns the others that the Master is in sight. When reading the play it is easy to forget that Sarah is there. However, her silent witness is an important factor to remember – she sees and hears everything. A flurry of activity follows, with Doalty causing his own particular kind of mayhem. The pupils concentrate on their several tasks as the focus shifts to Hugh's arrival. The false alarm only serves to heighten the moment when the big man at last appears. Friel's stage-directions are again significant. Hugh has consumed a large amount of drink at the christening but he is not drunk – his ability to remain partially sober suggests that he is aware of far more than he cares to acknowledge.

Hugh's arrival indicates a change of gear. The atmosphere is charged as Hugh's personality dominates the room. He treats his son like a servant, handing his coat, hat and stick to Manus '*as if to a footman*' (p. 21). Despite his down-at-heel appearance, he still retains the habits of a gentleman-scholar. Characterised by his elaborate speech he addresses the gathering in the manner previously the butt of Doalty's mimicry. Hugh is a formidable presence, intellectually arrogant but not without humour. He knows why Bridget is innocently questioning him about the name of Nellie Ruadh's baby and teases the class with his protracted answer. Again, the ritual of naming is brought to our attention. Hugh plays with Doalty, the class clown, turning his jokes against him and testing his weak point, mental arithmetic. All this produces merriment amongst the pupils but a tension returns when Hugh enquires about Sean Beag, Nora Dan and the Donnelly twins. This time Bridget is quick to suggest that the twins are collecting peat for the fires and changes the subject by offering to pay Hugh for her lessons.

The Donnelly twins are once more linked with news of subversive activity in the parish. After sending Manus off for strong, black tea (and an unceremonious shout later for a slice of soda bread), Hugh tells of his encounter with Captain Lancey of the Royal Engineers. He confirms that horses have strayed and equipment is missing (where is the pole that Doalty has brought with him? can Hugh see it or has Doalty hidden it somewhere in the room?), and has suggested that Lancey talks to the class himself. Hugh, with a metaphorical eyebrow raised, expresses his 'surprise' that Lancey can only speak English. His sardonic comment that English is best suited to the purposes of commerce shows his contempt for the paucity of the language and, by extension, the English nation. As he grandly imparts that Lancey 'acquiesced to my logic' (p. 23), Hugh fails to notice Maire's mounting impatience.

The spirited young woman gets '*uneasily but determinedly*' to her feet and announces that they 'should all be learning to speak English' (p. 24). Maire is brave here to speak out. She refers to O'Connell's belief that only with knowledge of the English language will the Irish people progress. Hugh fails to acknowledge that language develops where commerce and industry flourish. Commitment to Irish and the conjugation of classical tongues in a rural environment, however civilised, potentially results in stagnation. And a culture expressed only in Irish is doomed. Maire's speech causes considerable comment in the class, mainly about O'Connell's dubious morals. Hugh scathingly dismisses him as 'that little Kerry politician' – a sharp contrast to the more usual attribution of 'The Liberator'. Friel's stage-direction, that Manus '*reappears on the platform above*', occurs just before Maire announces that she needs English because she is to emigrate to America (p. 25). The timing of the re-appearance in an elevated position is crucial, as it isolates the character from the rest of the action and enables the audience to see more clearly the effect of Maire's bold statement on Manus. Hugh's response is to ignore her and seek refuge in his flask of whiskey.

Hugh continues by informing the class that he has met Mr George Alexander, Justice of the Peace, who offered him the post of headmaster of the new National School. This is probably not true but merely a ploy by Hugh to regain the upper hand. As Maire has implied earlier, notwithstanding his qualifications, Hugh's character and habitual drinking would probably prevent him getting the post. Moreover, it is very unlikely that Alexander would agree to Hugh's terms. There would be a fixed curriculum and all subjects, as Bridget has informed us, would be taught in English. However, Hugh speaks with such authority that it might as well be true. Effectively he is telling Maire and Manus that their relationship has no future. Hugh needs Manus to look after him and will use any means to keep him at home. We can imagine Manus motionless aloft. Maire sits, apparently defeated (p. 25). As a result of this petty triumph, Hugh chooses to relinquish the day and hands over the class to Manus, moving slowly towards the stairs. Everybody's attention is away from the door, the mood unsettled, each character dealing with his or her individual response to what has just transpired.

Owen's opening lines as he stands in the doorway rapidly switch the focus to the new character. His energy and charm transforms the atmosphere into a joyous homecoming, although Manus's reactions may be mixed – yet another factor threatens the status quo. Owen embraces Hugh *'warmly and genuinely'* – he certainly seems to know how to handle his father, although his suggestion that he should take Hugh out for both to get 'footless drunk' might be considered irresponsible (p. 27). And Manus does not appear to feature in Owen's plans for a good night out. Owen declares that nothing has changed, everything looks and smells the same, an ironic observation at a time when life in Baile Beag is about to be changed irrevocably. Owen's energy charges the room as he eagerly greets each person (with the exception of Sarah, who shyly hangs back), but his smart city clothes set him visually at odds with his surroundings. Owen clearly shares roots with the company onstage but at the same time looks an outsider. Maire and Bridget tease and question him about his reported wealth but Owen's response is evasive and he passes off their enquiries with a joke. The discrepancy between what Owen is and what he appears to be is an important one for us to note at this point.

Owen, in total command of the situation, gradually introduces the idea that he is involved with the military. He refers to Lancey and Yolland as his 'friends' and employs Hugh's game to identify their respective functions in the map-making and *'to involve his classroom audience'* (p. 29). Hugh invites the strangers in – 'Your friends are our friends' – and Owen moves towards the door. As the others scurry around tidying up to Hugh's urging, Owen spies Sarah and asks who she is. After a brief hesitation, Sarah responds to Owen's kindness (as she has to Manus's) and introduces herself, quite naturally stating her full name. Sarah attempts to share her achievement with Manus, but he is more concerned with Owen's announcement (made in the doorway on the point of exiting) that he is in the pay of the military. Enlistment, taking the King's shilling, could be construed by an Irishman as an act of treason. Waving aside Manus's blunt question as to whether he has enlisted, Owen admits that he is a translator.

Owen's 'delight' at returning home is genuine. He talks about being back amongst *civilised* people and treats everyone with an easy charm. He clearly enjoys entertaining the class, but how much is this a 'performance'? Might Owen be 'working' his audience, softening them up so that he can introduce his 'friends'? Underneath the gaiety of his greetings does he feel any guilt about returning home in such circumstances, and how hard has it been for him to present a relaxed and convivial persona? Friel indicates that Owen is courteous to everyone and everything he does is *invested with consideration and enthusiasm* (p. 26), but it is also evident that he has manipulated the situation to his advantage. Whatever his motives, he convincingly generates excitement and expectation – the rhythm of the scene has quickened and the focus sharpened since his entrance. His somewhat provocative exit-line – 'My job is to translate the quaint, archaic tongue you people persist in speaking into the King's good English' – is delivered with consummate skill and the appropriate measure of good humour so as not to cause offence. It would seem that Owen can get away with anything. Manus, however, has no such facility. While Hugh pours another drink (a tell-tale sign of discomfort, or is he fortifying himself to greet his guests?) and supervises the tidying of the room, Manus tries to confront Maire about her leaving. She will not be drawn, but turns on him accusing him of weakness and disloyalty to her. Maire's declaration that he now has nothing (perhaps not even her) and her cruel but realistic proposition that he can always 'Teach classics to the cows', sums up her despair (p. 31).

Lancey and Yolland are welcomed by Hugh in English – Friel indicates he '*becomes expansive, almost courtly*' – and, more elaborately, in Latin (p. 32). Remember that from now on when English is spoken both Hugh and Manus understand what is being said. Also imagine the impact of the soldiers' presence in the room. Visually they are sharply contrasted to the locals. Their uniforms look out of place, even incongruous, in the lowly barn. They also *sound* different, as they will speak with an English accent. Lancey refuses Hugh's offer of a drink, turning to Owen for support in his task of addressing the 'community'. Surprisingly, he refers to Owen as Roland, as does Yolland later in the scene. Is this a genuine mistake, a mishearing by the English soldiers, or has Owen introduced himself to them under an assumed name in order to get a job? Lancey launches into his explanation as to why the soldiers are in the area. Note the way Lancey, the colonist, speaks to the community and how his patronising manner provokes impolite sniggers from Doalty, Bridget and Sarah.

Owen quickly deals with the difficulty by suggesting that he translate into Irish. Lancey's information is specific. The map is to be on a large scale in order to give as much detail as possible. By implication, this would be of considerable use to an army of occupation should there be any trouble in 'this part of the Empire' (p. 34). Owen's translation is selective – giving rise initially to some humour – either because he feels the detail unnecessary or more likely because the locals might worry if they knew exactly what was going on. Lancey's quote from the White Paper is meant to reassure the Irish people that the map will be in the interest of the 'proprietors and occupiers' of the land. Owen deliberately mistranslates, as the probable outcome will result in greater hardship for the likes of the hedge-school scholars. Lancey's affirmation that 'Ireland is privileged' is met with approval by Hugh, who during Lancey's address has taken a fair amount of drink. However, he makes no comment on Owen's partial translation. Manus also remains silent, probably standing apart from the rest of the group.

Owen now calls upon Yolland to say a few words. Owen uses his Christian name, suggesting a degree of friendliness. Maire shows an interest in Yolland which Owen exaggerates in order to encourage the awkward soldier. Yolland's halting speech is rather engaging, although again Owen limits his translation to the essentials. Note that Yolland's apology for being a 'crude ... intrusion' on their lives is not translated. Hugh, now drunk, completes the formalities. He fulsomely welcomes the soldiers into his home, offering them 'friendship, our hospitality, and every assistance' (p. 36). Although Owen has stage-managed this meeting we should remember that Hugh readily acquiesces to the military presence. Perhaps the numbing effect of the drink facilitates this gesture of hospitality. The hosts and guests mingle as Owen moves to meet Manus.

Owen's opening gambit as the two brothers eye each other is to joke about Lancey's rigid manner, but he is careful to confirm that Yolland is 'alright'. Manus, however, cuts to the chase, confronting Owen with his imperfect translation. Owen is self-deprecating, trying to pass it off, but Manus persists. Owen's response is witty, suggesting that ambiguity in meaning is the beginning of poetry, but Manus knows what the map-making can lead to – a military operation. He also asserts that there is nothing wrong with the place-names, recognising the danger of their 'translation' into English. He also roundly berates Owen for allowing the soldiers to call him Roland. Owen's explanation is inadequate but he implies that Manus is making a fuss about nothing – the name may be different but he is 'the same me'. Manus's reply is deliberately ambiguous. The cut and thrust of the encounter hints at a friction between the two which has not been healed by time. Owen's comment that they 'complement each other' is meant to be a positive description of their relationship but it also implies two very different personalities with conflicting values and priorities. Owen dispels the tension with a light punch to Manus as he moves '*confidently across the floor*' to introduce Maire to Yolland (p. 37).

The stage-picture at the end of the act is important for you to consider as it summarises the action so far. Owen takes Maire by the hand and introduces her to his friend George, thus fulfilling his function as 'the go-between' in another guise. Hugh, very drunk, tries to climb the stairs, seeking the refuge of his bed and oblivion. Jimmy returns to Homer, lost in the realms of antiquity. Doalty and Bridget giggle. Sarah stares at Manus, who probably watches Maire enjoy the attentions of Yolland and Owen. The distance between Sarah and Manus is in marked contrast to their intimacy at the beginning of the act. Friel does not mention Lancey, who is still in the room, possibly standing slightly apart, waiting to leave. The main players are all gathered. The act ends on an upbeat, again fuelled by Owen's energy, but discernible tensions have been revealed and the presence of the soldiers is unsettling.

Act Two, Scene One

MAP-MAKING Several days have passed and it is evident from the large map, reference books and other paraphernalia strewn on the floor that Owen and Yolland are well advanced in the work. They have taken over the barn – in a sense they have occupied it. The image is a powerful one; the washing hanging on the makeshift clothes-line reminds us that this is also a home but the main focus of attention is the soldiers' work. Owen and Yolland are strongly contrasted. Owen is active and absorbed, Yolland languid and preoccupied. Friel's note about Yolland's ease as opposed to his hesitancy in the previous act is important – 'he is at home here now'. He is pleasantly drowsy, slowly succumbing to the combined effect of the heat of the late-afternoon sun and the potency of the poteen. Friel also identifies the 'Name-Book', simply a prop at this point but one which will take on symbolic significance as the story unfolds.

The opening exchange between Owen and Yolland establishes the precise nature of their task – 'we are trying to denominate and at the same time describe . . .' (p. 40). It also shows the detail in which the map is being made – every stream and beach, however small, is being recorded. It is interesting that the names have been 'translated' before and that there is no consistency in their naming in the various reference books. This gives Owen further justification for the work in which he is involved. Although Yolland is complimentary about Owen's developing skills it is clear that his own mind is not really on the job in hand. He is pleased with himself, however, at the way he stood up to Lancey. In all respects Yolland is feeling more at ease. Note carefully exactly when Manus enters – in time to overhear Yolland's 'But certain tasks demand their own tempo. You cannot rename a whole country overnight' (p. 41). Manus continues to refuse to speak to Yolland in English and, as he gathers the washing, witnesses Owen enthusiastically engaged in his work and the easy familiarity between the two men.

Yolland's offer of the oranges is made in a spirit of friendliness but comes over in an unintentionally patronising way – the coloniser dispensing largess to the natives. Manus perceives Yolland as the colonial but cannot, however, quite make him out. He is not the stereotypical soldier, there is something different about Yolland: is it his innocence, his concern not to intrude, his basic decency? Manus understands the Lanceys of this world but Yolland is an enigma. He is quite sure, however, about his brother: 'there are always the Rolands' – he might as well have said 'Judas'. Remember, only Owen hears this and he is careful not to disclose it to Yolland. Instead he refers to Manus's earlier rebuke regarding the bottle of poteen. Manus's concern for his father is evident, as is his attitude towards Owen's lack of thought. The tension between the brothers is palpably manifest onstage, with Owen obviously trying to protect his friend George from any embarrassment.

There follows some revealing information concerning Manus and Hugh. The accident caused by the father leading to the son's disability results in a reversal of roles. The son's misplaced guilt informs his relationship with his father. The absence of the mother means that Manus is not only fulfilling his obligations as (over)dutiful son but has also assumed the responsibilities of a wife. If the accident happened because Hugh was drunk, then his habit is well over twenty years old. Responding to Yolland's question about Manus's 'salary', Owen uses the word 'throws' rather than 'gives' (p. 43), as one might do to a beggar. Hugh is on the poverty-line himself – his earnings from the hedge-school are inevitably erratic – but it is his attitude which is offensive. We have already seen Hugh treat Manus like a servant so we have no reason to doubt Owen's assessment. Owen congratulates himself on getting out in time, but his return home is hardly auspicious.

Yolland starts to talk about the things which are preoccupying him, his reference to the locals' hostility perhaps unconsciously prompted by Manus's manner. The little girl's gesture has made an impression on him and he is anxious to know more about the Donnelly twins (p. 44). This is the third time they have been mentioned, their significance increasing on each occasion. Lancey wants them for questioning, they are now identified as marked men. Owen's response, or lack of it, is interesting here. He has been away from Baile Beag for six years, during which time the Donnelly twins, already famous for their prowess as fishermen, may have become infamous for their involvement with Fenian resistance. If Owen is innocent of this knowledge then what he says can be taken at face value. But if he knows or even suspects that the Donnelly twins are involved in subversive activities then his evasion could be seen as an instinctive protection of his own people, or he could be simply biding his time until he has more information.

THE LITANY Yolland gazes out of the window towards Maire's house. He is clearly interested in Maire and Owen

BRIAN FRIEL

encourages him to 'drop in' and join the musical evening.
Does Owen realise that Maire is Manus's 'intended'? – if
so, then this is a careless, even cruel, suggestion. Owen
may, however, simply be encouraging the soldiers to mix
with the locals and be looking out for his friend George.
Suddenly the scene lifts into a heightened moment as
Owen speaks the Irish place-names in response to
Yolland's request (p. 45). There is a change in rhythm
and pace, the stage stills and time seems to stretch as
Owen unconsciously creates a litany out of the names.
The effect is subtle and achieved almost subliminally.
Yolland asks if he could live in Baile Beag. The word 'live'
in this context does not just mean to be domiciled in a
particular place but also to be 'alive' in it. Owen's
response is pragmatic and dismissive. Ironically equating
Baile Beag to Eden, Owen accuses Yolland of being 'a
bloody romantic' who 'wouldn't survive a mild winter' in
such circumstances (p. 45).

Doalty's entrance '*in a rush*' interrupts their conversation and breaks the mood (p. 45). Doalty is a messenger
breezily bringing news that forwards the plot, but it is his
offstage action which carries the greater significance. His
brief appearance reminds Yolland of Doalty's 'act of
kindness' towards him that morning. Yolland's interpretation is benign, but Doalty could as easily be pin-
pointing Yolland's tent for others. This can be a chilling
moment in the theatre as the implications of Doalty's
seemingly innocent action (as it might well be) are
gradually absorbed. Owen makes no comment. Yolland,
still considering a life in Ballybeg – as he calls it – embarks
on a little autobiography, revealing details of his life and
his relationship with his father. Yolland is an officer in the
British Army by default. He does not respond immedi-

ately to Owen's question about fate, but whereas he believes fate might have been kind to him by bringing him to Ballybeg it has, ironically, dealt him a deadly hand.

Lancey reminds Yolland of his father. It is important that the audience recognises Lancey as a perfect colonial servant, efficient, hard-working, altogether excellent at his job. He shares with Yolland's father 'that drive ... that dedication; that indefatigable energy' that builds empires and which Yolland so singularly lacks (p. 47). Yolland knows that he does not have his father's coherence nor does he share his belief. Yolland struggles to answer Owen's question about fate by trying to define his feelings towards Baile Beag — as he now calls it — where he thinks he could 'live'. Owen sardonically sees it as a retrograde step — 'Back into ancient time?' — but Yolland perceives it as 'experience being of a totally different order', that he 'had moved into a consciousness that wasn't striving nor agitated, but at its ease and with its own conviction and assurance'. He recognises, however, that he could never really belong — the 'language of the tribe' would 'always elude' him, 'the private core' would remain 'hermetic' (p. 48).

WORDS ARE NOT IMMORTAL Hugh, in the full flow of his Latin text, immediately spots the bottle of poteen — it is as instinctive as breathing. Friel's description emphasises his *jaunty and alert* manner to the point of self-parody. Hugh is giving a 'performance', adopting a persona to play to a gallery of one — Yolland. Owen may also be part of the audience but he knows all the routines and is not so easily impressed. The role-playing provides a critical distance from Hugh's pronouncements. Owen calls him 'pompous', Yolland considers him 'astute'. He seems to be the former but his analysis of the psyche and condition of the Irish people suggests the latter. His arrogance is evident, however: he thinks Wordsworth should have heard of him; he 'overlooks' Britain, feeling closer to the 'warm Mediterranean' and its classical tongues, thus contributing to the death of his own language; and he regards the priest as his intellectual inferior yet needs his good offices in order to get the job at the new National School. He is also selfish, thinking only of his own needs in this regard. Manus does not appear to feature in his plans (pp. 49–51).

Yolland brings the conversation round to the nature of the Irish language, his eager questions prompting Hugh's discourse. This is the crux of the play's argument. Hugh affirms that the Irish like to think they are surrounded by truths and that the richness of their language and literature compensates for the material poverty of their daily lives. He also suggests that the Irish are a spiritual people, although there does not seem much evidence of this in the play. Owen '*not unkindly*' reminds him that changes are taking place and, using the place-names as an example, wryly asks, 'Will you be able to find your way?' (p. 51). True to form, Hugh takes a drink instead of replying directly. His next comment is made to Yolland but is, in a way, an oblique response to his son. Hugh recognises 'the mythologies of fantasy and hope and self-deception' inherent in the language and culture, and suggests it is a defence against 'inevitabilities'. He then swiftly changes the subject, tone and reflective mood of the conversation by asking his son for a loan – in fact more than Owen's daily pay (p. 72) – and announcing the grand title of his new book. This demonstration of Hugh's quick wit – has the title been made up on the spur of the moment? – and the self-mocking admission that it is 'the best part of the enterprise', suggests it is a fantasy and that the book will never be written.

Hugh acknowledges that he is interrupting important work and goes to leave. However, he stops at the door – a focal point in the room – to deliver the central speech of the play. Using a coded image, created in perfect accord with the 'work of moment', Hugh warns that words are not 'immortal' and that a civilisation can be 'imprisoned' in a language and mindset which fails to recognise the forces of change. At the end of the speech Hugh pauses for a moment, allowing the thought to hang in the air, then with a courteous 'Gentlemen', he is gone. The pace changes after his exit, both men responding differently to Hugh's interpretation of the 'facts'. Owen maintains that his father is pompous and obstinate; but Hugh's words have also touched on a concern that has been worrying Yolland since his arrival in Baile Beag. He is unhappy about his part in 'what's happening', gradually recognising it to be 'an eviction of sorts'. Yolland uses a word that has a particular resonance for the Irish – an act of dispossession. In the sharp exchange that follows – Owen defending their position, Yolland doubting its wisdom – the characters' lines overlap one another denoting its urgency and pace. Yolland has the final word though – 'Something is being eroded' (p. 53).

TOBAIR VREE Owen's response is the story of Tobair Vree. His point is clear – why keep the name if nobody knows its origin, the story is no longer told or even remembered. Owen turns the word 'eroded' back on Yolland but he loses the argument. Yolland asserts his authority and insists that the name remains. The fact that

Owen remembers the story is sufficient reason to keep it (p. 53). But implicit in this sequence is the idea that stories must be repeated, or else they are gone forever, just as language must be kept alive or renewed or it and the culture are irredeemably lost. Whether or not it is this discussion, which focuses on naming and identity, that moves Owen to renounce his adopted name of Roland, the combative mood certainly provides the opportunity. At first he '*Explodes*', breaking the tension, then pulls back to '*softly*' announce his name. Yolland's stunned response builds into another sequence which again 'explodes' with their laughter. The energy, pace and timing of these passages are effective and engaging, also serving to consolidate the natural friendship between the two men (p. 54). Here the boundaries of class, culture and tribe appear to be overcome as Owen and Yolland revel in their task of christening the country – the new Eden. But this accord is only possible because Owen has bought into the British operation. We are reminded of this by Manus's appearance – the conscience of the community (p. 55).

Manus is reluctant to share his news with the 'colonial', but eventually acquiesces to Owen's pleading. At last Yolland feels included and naturally extends his friendship to Manus. The handshake between the British soldier and the Irish scholar is an important visual image and the shared toast is also significant. But the celebrations and Manus's euphoria at the prospect of being his own master at £42 a year are tinged with irony. We know that the army will soon reach the island, as will the National School system, so his hedge-school on Inis Meadhon is effectively doomed. Maire's lack of enthusiasm for Manus's news is evident and, as he disappears upstairs, her attention shifts to George. Friel states, '*Maire moves away, touching the text book with her toe.*' Standing apart from the two men her movement is coquettish as she nonchalantly mentions the Fiddler O'Shea and the dance. The instant he hears 'Tobair Vree' Yolland joins in the exchange. Maire and Yolland's eagerness to communicate and Owen's attempt at translation makes for a very funny sequence. It has to be achieved at high speed for maximum effect. Interestingly, Maire is more sure-footed in this exchange, Yolland continually resorting to his characteristic 'Sorry-sorry?', as though he were not only unable to understand but also in a perpetual state of apology (pp. 59–60).

Owen, heartlessly, tells Manus to take over when he descends with the empty can. How much Manus is aware of the growing empathy between Maire and Yolland is debatable, but he is obviously left stranded as Maire asks Owen for a drink. Yolland, *'intoxicated'* by the poteen, the heady atmosphere of Eden, the close presence of Maire, and the prospect of the dance, brings the scene to its climax. Consider the image: Yolland raised on the stool shouting his head off; Owen, getting on for 'footless' by this time, congratulating Yolland on his 'Perfect' pronunciation; Maire joining in the festivities, possibly laughing at the two inebriates; and Manus, sober and isolated, watching them. Friel asks for the reel music to be introduced to top Yolland's final 'bloody marvellous'. Imagine the sound and feel the energy of the reel as it sustains the momentum of the scene and projects us forward in time during the blackout as we segue into the offstage dance (p. 61).

Act Two, Scene Two
THE LEAP ACROSS THE DITCH This is a perfectly structured scene. Time is compressed, a day has passed,

but the dramatic impetus of the action demands continuity. Friel suggests that the scene should be played in the foreground, losing as much of the schoolroom as possible by lighting. We are, therefore, transported out into the countryside, perhaps onto a moonlit headland, with the sea on the horizon and, as the weather is holding, the harvest moon visible in the distance. The night is warm and the mood romantic. As the music reaches a crescendo, Maire and Yolland can be seen running, hand-in-hand, exhilarated by the dance which they have just left. As they arrive onstage the music fades to an appropriate level and eventually ceases. Friel indicates that it is replaced by guitar music, but natural sounds would be equally appropriate if subtly introduced.

Look carefully at the first four lines. If you did not know that one character was speaking Irish and the other English, you might think that Maire and Yolland were having a conversation. There seems to be an inspirational form of communication between them, reflected in their uninhibited physicality. Maire speaks of the 'leap across the ditch' – an important metaphor signifying the young lovers' imaginative leap across the tribal and class boundaries that divide them. Now consider how the next four lines of dialogue might be delivered, taking into account Friel's precise stage-directions – language and communication start to breakdown as they become more aware of each other and they drift farther apart. The exchange about the wet grass and Maire's wet feet shows how differently they perceive the same phenomenon. The balance of the sentences heightens the contrast (p. 62).

'ALWAYS' The lovers' frustration as they struggle to communicate is a kind of sweet anguish for them but a source of comedy for the audience. Maire tries Latin but to no avail – Yolland thinks she is still speaking Gaelic – and then hits on her three words of English which she told Jimmy about in Act One. Yolland recognises two of the three elements but is stumped by the third, probably because the Irish do not pronounce 'th'. When he finally understands he praises Maire's 'Perfect English' (p. 64). Maire's next translation elicits such an excited response from Yolland that she thinks her Aunt Mary has taught her something sexually provocative. Yolland, however, is so concerned to latch on to anything that might conceivably enable communication that he fails to recognise Maire's English sentence as a text-book phrase. We do, however, learn a little more about Yolland's background. Now follow the stage-directions carefully; Friel is very precise: movement and stillness, language and silence combine to create a rhythm and image in which actors and audience share an imaginative space.

Yolland and Maire develop Owen's litany of names into an antiphonal duet. It is again a heightened moment although more emotionally charged. The length of the names shorten as they meet suggesting a slight quickening of the pace. Note that it is Maire who holds out her hands to Yolland, she takes the initiative. In a way she has been moving towards this moment ever since her entrance in the previous scene. I am not implying that she has been deliberately calculating or manipulative, but she is more strong-willed and spirited than Yolland has ever dared to be. As they embrace, the language becomes sensual. Maire feels the softness of his 'gentleman's' hands – remember the blisters on her peasant's hands from the harvesting – and recalls the whiteness of the skin on his shoulders as she watched him wash outside his tent every morning.

Yolland, too, has been watching Maire and longs to tell her how beautiful she is. They both 'tremble' at the other's touch and in those three lines it appears as though they fully understand one another – but the communication is physical and imaginative rather than intellectual. Maire takes his face in her hands and it is then that they articulate what each desire. The ironic twist at the end of the scene reveals that this potential union is based on different perceptions and, despite the reiteration of 'always', it is evident that their love will be short-lived.

As the couple embrace and kiss we should again consider the stage-picture. Here is a local Irish girl in the arms of a British soldier – a romantic but also a shocking image suggesting conquest, collaboration, colonisation. Sarah's stunned response is expressed on a more personal level. Her one thought is to tell Manus as she repeats his name. As she runs off into the night a further irony emerges – we know that Sarah will seek Manus out and speak of what she has seen. Manus, with care and patience, has given her language and with it Sarah will tell him of Maire's betrayal. Friel indicates that the music reaches a crescendo as the scene fades on Maire and Yolland. The combination of elements creates a powerful ending, but the whole scene has a tremendous impact and constitutes the emotional climax of the play – what happens after is the anti-climactic consequence of Maire and Yolland's transgression.

Act Three

The weather has broken. Eden is blighted. Both Owen and Sarah are agitated, neither able to work. Sarah is 'more waiflike than ever' (p. 68). When Manus emerges from above he is very focused, moving with determination and urgency, but his emotional state is soon revealed as the overloaded bag breaks. As Owen leaps to his brother's assistance and runs upstairs for his travelling bag, Sarah tries to speak to Manus but he ignores her. It is important in all this activity to be aware of the emotional current of the scene. The manner of Manus's preparations for departure suggests that he is in turmoil. The audience does not yet know why. Also, when he reappears with the bag, Owen claims that he's 'finished with it', implying that he will not be travelling again.

In the exchange between Manus and Owen we learn that Yolland is missing and that a search party is out looking for him (p. 70). Owen tries to persuade Manus to stay – perhaps George's absence is only temporary, and a hasty departure points to Manus's involvement in his disappearance. Manus confesses his ineptitude. He *had* gone looking for Yolland full of vengeance, with a stone in his hand intending 'to fell him'. But faced with the sight of him and Maire together all he could manage was an ineffectual shout in Irish. Ashamed, Manus acknowledges his stupidity: 'The wrong gesture in the wrong language'. Manus is in a state of emotional shock, caused by Maire's cruel betrayal and his own potential for violence. What is motivating his flight – anger, hurt, shame, fear? Or is he sacrificing himself for the sake of the community by drawing attention and resources away from the townland? He refuses to see Lancey, even to clear himself. He seems intent on keeping his job open in Inis Meadhon but he may be heading for their mother's cousins in Mayo – his plans are vague. All he wants to do is get out.

Before he leaves he does two things. First, he sets his house in order. He itemises everything he does for his father in the hope that Owen will take over the

responsibility. This gives a very interesting insight into the
father and son's life together and confirms the amount of
time Manus has devoted to Hugh's needs. He takes only
the books that belong to him – the comment about the pet
lamb shows that he puts learning before sentimentality –
and refuses Owen's offer of money. They part with a
formal handshake, no fraternal embrace. Second, he
makes sure that Sarah is emotionally independent and can
manage without him. Lacking any apparent warmth of
concern he goes through the lesson of Act One, affirming
that 'There's nothing to stop you now – nothing in the
wide world.' The repeated and rhythmic, 'It's alright – it's
alright – you did no harm – you did no harm at all,' and
the kiss on the top of her head is an act of forgiveness,
absolving Sarah of any guilt. Manus deflects his own
emotion into these rituals of leaving and absolution. He
has no word for Maire. But he is not denied the audience's
sympathy. This is the longest sequence involving Manus
as the foregrounded character, and it is important that we
are granted this confirmation of his qualities late on in the
play. His honesty and confusion are very human and we
know that something rare is lost to the community by his
departure. His lameness may symbolise the community's
spiritual deprivation but here is a good man. Owen and
Sarah instinctively know this as he leaves (pp. 72–3).

GREAT CRACK Sarah, too upset to answer Owen, resorts
to mime in response to his question as to Hugh's
whereabouts. It is the same mime she gave to Manus in
Act One – he interpreted correctly but Owen is unfamiliar
with her ways and he, and therefore the audience, cannot
understand her. Bridget and Doalty's riotous arrival
swiftly changes the solemn mood. Friel describes them

as 'self-consciously noisier, more ebullient, more garrulous than ever – brimming over with excitement and gossip and brio', as though they are aware of their roles as messengers in the great drama that is unfolding around them. They give a vivid account of the army's reinforcements cutting a swathe through the surrounding fields. They have no sympathy for Barney Petey whose crop is ruined, and delight in Hugh and Jimmy roaring defiance at the British force. Bridget and Doalty are having the time of their lives, for them it is great crack, the real danger not yet apparent. Bridget mentions that Hugh is at a wake – the first time we hear of a death and the subject of Sarah's mime earlier – and is in no state to take a class. The mood slowly turns to one of anxiety as they realise that Manus is gone (pp. 74–5).

It is interesting to speculate what the characters witnessed the previous evening. Bridget and Doalty know more than they are at first prepared to tell. When pressed, Bridget names the Donnelly twins and Doalty confirms that their boat disappeared after the dance. Could this mean that Yolland's body has been dumped out at sea? When Doalty speaks of Yolland it is in the past tense (p. 76). Owen knows that Lancey will question him. How will he respond? As the go-between in the army's pay he will be expected to co-operate with the British. As George's friend he has a personal interest in the lieutenant's welfare. But his own brother is now implicated and it is becoming clear that the locals do not altogether trust him. Doalty's 'sudden excessive interest in the scene outside' marks the end of his willingness to answer Owen's questions.

MAIRE'S GRIEF Maire has come seeking news of Yolland. Owen is polite but non-committal and it is difficult to determine precisely his attitude towards her. Significantly, she kneels on the floor where Owen had the big map earlier and starts to trace another, as Yolland had done in the wet sand the night before. Maire remembers the evening with a vivid intensity and she carefully recites the old Anglo-Saxon place-names with their strange sounding poetry. Yolland's world has replaced her own – 'I have it all in my head now.' She knows instinctively that 'something very bad's happened to him' (p. 78).

Maire is, of course, the focus of attention throughout her long speech and her *'acute distress'* will arouse sympathy in the audience. But what of the other characters onstage? Neither Sarah nor Owen, both of whom she directly addresses, respond to her. And Bridget and Doalty remain silent. Why does no one comfort her? Are they embarrassed by her distress? Or does their silence convey an explicit condemnation of her liaison with the British soldier? Is this the community ostracising Maire? Sarah, Bridget and Doalty are all fond of Manus and he has fled, the victim of Maire's betrayal. Owen 'the outsider' may have mixed feelings. However, by the end of the speech, Maire is isolated, alone. Her ignorant but innocent remark about Brooklyn is touching and her rueful comment about the short life of Nellie Ruadh's baby could equally apply to her brief glimpse of happiness. Think about this section carefully; it is easy to forget when reading the play that the other four characters are in the room watching Maire, but it is through their presence and silent response that Maire's anguish is put into some kind of critical perspective.

'EDICTUM IMPERATORIS' The silence is sustained after Maire's exit. The focus switches to Manus. Doalty's image of him limping along the coast hunted by the army 'like bloody beagles' is an acknowledgement that his chances of evading capture are slim – 'They'll overtake him before night for Christ's sake' (p. 79). Lancey's brisk entrance, '*now the commanding officer*', switches the focus back to Yolland. Lancey's announcement is clear enough. Owen is overwhelmed by the power that is about to be unleashed. Moreover, he is humiliated in front of his fellow countrymen and women, forced to interpret Lancey's instructions accurately. When Lancey comes to the list of names that Owen has so diligently translated, the betrayer is betrayed. Owen has no status, he is a journeyman translator in the pay of the British, obliged to tell his own people that if Yolland is not found their townlands will be razed to the ground. As Lancey and Owen come to the end of the list the violation is complete. Owen uses the word 'ravish' advisedly (p. 81).

Lancey turns his attention to the community represen-tatives. We are aware of Sarah's symbolic significance at this point, but here I want you to consider her position in human terms. Sarah has not spoken since Manus left, one of the townlands named by Lancey was hers, she is now in direct confrontation with him, and her terror robs her of speech. Owen answers for her. Note that Lancey makes Owen use the Anglicised form of 'Bun na hAdhann' and later 'Tulach Alainn' in recognition of his and Britain's authority. Owen lies about Manus's whereabouts, Doalty helping him out by distracting Lancey's attention to the burning camp. Lancey departs, leaving the two men in no doubt as to the ferocity of British retribution if Yolland is not found.

It is important, however, not to demonise Lancey. He is in charge of a large number of men, one of whom is missing. Guerilla activities have escalated and he has every reason to believe that his force's safety is threatened. There are precedents for Lancey's action and in his view he is perfectly justified in taking such retaliatory measures. Remember also Yolland's description in Act Two of Lancey's exemplary behaviour in the camp. However, he *is* the perfect colonial servant, convinced of the rightness of his mission, and as a professional member of the imperial machine is therefore implicated in the malign effect of British involvement in Ireland. Some of the responsibility for the chaos that has erupted in Ballybeg must lie with Yolland. He allowed his heart to rule his head, his love affair with the country extending naturally to Maire. However, Yolland is '*a soldier by accident*', and as an individual is critical of the British presence in Ireland, certainly disturbed about his part in it. His shyness and awkward manner are appealing, his unselfconscious sensitivity towards the local people is laudable, and his concern to preserve the Irish language and culture is indisputable. He knows instinctively that he is the real 'barbarian' in Ballybeg (see pp. 90–91). But his innocence and romanticism are also dangerous. His unthinking 'leap across the ditch' with Maire has probably killed him and may well result in the deaths of many more.

Bridget, Sarah and Doalty are contrasted in their response to Lancey's manner and edict. Bridget's instinct is flight. She is still practical but panics when she thinks she smells the potato blight (p. 83). Her relief – 'God, I thought we were destroyed altogether' – ironically foreshadows the great Famine that was to hit the country a decade later. Sarah, despite Owen's gentle reassurance, is stoical and stubbornly refuses to believe that her speech will return. In fact she shakes her head twice, the second time '*slowly, emphatically*', and then '*she smiles at Owen.*' This extraordinary gesture at a time of trauma is possibly a sign of acceptance of her condition. Doalty's reaction is to fight. He has remained behind to speak privately to Owen. In the short exchange between them there is an implicit understanding as to what has happened to Yolland and that the key to effective action lies with the Donnelly twins (p. 84). Owen is non-committal but Doalty's instinct is to trust him as a fellow Irishman. Doalty's reference to British reprisals when his grandfather was a boy puts the immediate situation into an historical perspective, suggesting also that the cycle of violence is recurring.

THE NAME-BOOK Owen, after a brief hesitation, leaves the precious Name-Book on the floor where it has fallen and goes upstairs to prepare for trouble. The two drunken Irishmen take the stage, their separate thought-processes evident: Hugh is outraged that Bartley Timlin from Cork has been appointed Master at the new National School; Jimmy is fixated on his proposed 'marriage' to Athene. There is some comic relief here, but the scene is underpinned by Hugh's futile anger and Jimmy's grotesque rapture. Hugh sees Timlin as an outsider and beneath contempt but his verdict on the hapless 'bacon-curer' – 'I am a barbarian in this place because I am not understood by anyone' – could equally apply to other characters in the play, most obviously Yolland who is outside the culture. Owen is, however, also an outsider, an exile from his townland and a betrayer of his country. Friel places this quotation at a point where Owen is slowly shifting his position towards recognising and openly acknowledging his complicity with the colonists.

Hugh watches Jimmy's pathetic display and his total withdrawal into a fantasy world which shields him from the reality of loneliness and isolation. Hugh instinctively produces his flask – the salve which protects him from his own demons – but his attention is caught by the Name-Book, which he picks up *'and leafs through, pronouncing the strange names as he does'*. This coincides with Owen's entrance from above with tea for Hugh and Jimmy. Owen *'snatches'* the Name-Book in the midst of Hugh's recital and *'throws'* it onto the table. The aggression implicit in these gestures is juxtaposed with Owen's *'apology'* to his father as he dismisses the 'catalogue of names', acknowledges his 'mistake' and claims that it has 'nothing to do with us' (p. 87). But Hugh responds immediately by telling Owen, and his Irish audience, that, 'We must learn those new names ... We must learn where we live. We must learn to make them our own. We must make them our new home.' Owen, stung by the use of the evocative and powerful world 'home', asserts, 'I know where I live.' But Hugh undermines Owen's position as the reconstituted Irishman by reminding him, and his Irish audience, 'that it is not the literal past, the "facts" of history, that shape us, but images of the past embodied in language'. He uses James – note the respectful use of the full name – as an example of someone who has 'ceased to make that discrimination'. Hugh reinforces his point by stating that the images must be constantly renewed otherwise we ossify.

Owen challenges his father to face the unsaid 'C', the 'unalterable fact' of eviction. Owen has taken over Manus's role at home and leaves to seek out Doalty – like Manus he has nothing to say to Lancey and we can only presume that he will join with his neighbours in defending what little they have. Hugh calls after Owen to take care, followed by the cryptic, 'To remember everything is a form of madness.' Is Hugh saying here that we must learn to forget the past otherwise we should all go mad? Certainly the stage-directions, where Hugh *'looks around the room, carefully, as if he were about to leave it forever'*, suggest that he is coming to terms with his past in order to face the present. He embarks on his longest speech in the play where he recalls himself and James setting out on their great adventure (pp. 88–9). The first two-thirds of the speech has a wonderfully buoyant rhythm to match the image of the 'two young gallants ... striding across the fresh green land' and the notion that 'Everything seemed to find definition that spring – a congruence, a miraculous matching of hope and past and present and possibility ... the rhythms of perception heightened. The whole enterprise of consciousness accelerated.' He speaks of his wife for the first time and his infant son, Manus, and now we perceive Hugh not as the arrogant, irascible old schoolmaster that he has become, but a young poet with a family to protect, and an ideal for which to fight. There is talk of gods and heroism but the magnificence fades as the poetry of the past asserts its own pull on their imaginations and they return home to 'Athens'. Perhaps we should consider that both visions are romantic and equally susceptible to false truths. Hugh concludes by confessing his confusion, which he shares with his friend.

The focus switches to Maire as she enters, instinctively drawn to the place where Yolland says he was happiest. Hugh offers to teach Maire English but he is aware that knowledge of the mechanics of the language will not necessarily ensure accurate translation, nor establish real communication. But he recognises that they must try because 'it's all we have' (p. 90). Maire asks him the meaning of the English word 'always'. Hugh dismisses it as 'a silly word' – nothing lasts forever. The funeral of Nellie Ruadh's baby is there to remind us that Maire and Yolland's happiness lasted only as briefly as the baby's life. The death is also symbolic of the vanished hope that was so positively, but ironically, expressed at the beginning of the play by Manus to Sarah – he has since fled, she has retreated into silence, dumb again. Jimmy wakes up and sits beside Maire, who has the Name-Book in her lap (p. 90). In his delusion, Jimmy speaks of his situation with Athene, which mirrors that of Maire and Yolland, advising her and us of the destructive anger which results from the 'casual' crossing of these tribal borders. The surreal context within which this idea is expressed does not diminish its resonance.

In his elevated position, Hugh is metaphorically placed between past and present. He is a traditional figure and yet recognises the imperative to change. He begins to intone a passage from Virgil's *Aeneid* which is itself a translation of Homer's *Odyssey*. He starts in Latin but translates into English/Irish. Is the translation for the audience's benefit or is it Hugh's way of 'renewing the images of the past'? Whatever the intention, Hugh is unable to remember the original, although he says he knows it 'backways' (pp. 90–91). The story is one of imperial ambition resulting in the destruction of a city. As Ballybeg is being razed to the ground and fire rages through the British camp, Hugh seems to be trying to stem the tide of destruction by the grandiloquence of his language, but, like some ancient king in mortal combat, he is losing the battle. He struggles back to the beginning of the story in an attempt to hold on to the fading memory, but the effect as the lights begin to dim is of Hugh receding into some kind of limbo where silence reigns. The final image is of Maire and Jimmy lost in their own kind of madness and Hugh poised on the edge of uncertainty.

Endnote

Translations raises many more questions than it answers. At the end of the play we know nothing for certain except that the future for those left in Ballybeg will be bleak. We also know with the wisdom of hindsight that the troubles caused by the British presence will intensify and the legacy of the relationship between Britain and Ireland still remains unresolved. The story by now is a familiar one, but the brilliance of the play lies in its telling. It touches us because Friel is able to pinpoint and show the historical moment through the lives of ordinary people. There are no heroes or villains – it is more complicated than that. We identify with the characters' dilemmas and recognise their frailties. What would we do in such circumstances? At the same time the playwright provides us with the critical perspective to see how the historical process is working and what questions to ask of it. In this way the play makes an important contribution to the debate. Friel is talking to the Irish people for sure, but the play has a powerful resonance that transcends national boundaries. *Translations* is an exhilarating experience in the theatre – it moves us deeply but also makes us think; it is about the death of a language and yet language is vibrant and alive onstage; and it addresses a seemingly intractable problem with compassion and humanity. It confirms a belief that the theatre can transform.

Textual Notes

2 *Homer* – (c. 700 BC) Greek epic poet.

3 Jimmy/James – Manus refers to 'Jimmy' to denote familiarity but to show respect or deference he also calls him James.

4 Athene – Greek virgin goddess of wisdom and warfare and daughter of Zeus. According to myth Athene sprang fully armed from the King of the God's forehead.

– Ulysses – Latin name for Odysseus. Jimmy is reading Homer's *Odyssey*, the epic poem which describes the ten-year journey of Odysseus from the siege of Troy back to Penelope, his wife, waiting patiently at home in Ithaca.

– wallet – a knapsack or pedlar's pack.

– tight one – mean.

– couldn't watch her – she's unpredictable.

5 Grania/Diarmuid – Grania, a beautiful young woman, falls in love with Diarmuid and runs away with him in order to escape the embrace of Finn MacCool, an old man.

– Artemis – Greek virgin goddess of the hunt and the moon. A daughter of Zeus.

– Helen of Troy – Helen is a daughter of Zeus and the mortal queen of Sparta, Leda. She married Menelaus, King of Sparta, but was abducted by Paris, prince of Troy, who was dazzled by her beauty. Menelaus led an army to Troy to get her back, which caused the Trojan War.

– jigged-up – sexually aroused.

9 Diana – Roman goddess of hunting and chastity. footering about – wasting time.

9 Poll na gCaorach – Hole for the Sheep.
10 sapper – a private in the Royal Engineers.
– Vesperal salutations – Good evening. Doalty is imitating Hugh, but it is a good example of elaborate speech.
– full as a pig – full of drink.
11 *Ignari, stulti, rustici* – Doalty is still imitating the Master, who is using Latin to insult the local peasants.
– pot-boys – youth who serves beer in a pub.
– whelps – puppies.
– on the batter – out and about.
– aul fella – father.
– Red Coats – British soldiers.
– Cnoc na Mona – Hill of Turf.
– lug – carry; it suggests that the machine is heavy. theodolite – surveying instrument for measuring angles.
– etymology – branch of philology concerned with the origin and derivation of words.
– yoke – shaped wooden harness.
– aul eejit – old idiot.
– Cripes – slang for Christ.
12 aul shaft – thick stick that is moved up and down inside the churn to turn milk into butter; Doalty is being slightly suggestive here.
– headline – main topic written at the top of the slate.
– Big Hughie – 'Mor' in Hugh's full name translates as 'big'. Hughie is a familiar form of Hugh, so Bridget is being mildly disrespectful.
13 Nellie Ruadh – red-haired Nellie.
– Horace – (65–8 BC) Latin poet celebrated for his satires.

14 Virgil – (70–19 BC) Roman poet.

 – *Georgics* – Virgil wrote four books on farming between 37–30 BC.

15 go and take a running race at yourself – have some sense.

 – Machaire Buide – Yellow Plain.

 – a dose – nuisance or worse; not a complimentary term.

16 ate me – be angry.

18 St Colmcille – Dove of the Curch.

 – lug – ear; 'beag', meaning small, could be pronounced 'bug', hence the rhyme.

19 yella meal – a kind of porridge.

20 jouk – sneak.

 – bugger – so-and-so; a colloquial term of abuse, often as not tinged with affection.

21 libations – act of pouring out wine as a religious offering.

 – Pliny Minor – (62–113) Roman writer noted for his letters.

22 Sophocles – (494–406 BC) Greek dramatist who wrote *Oedipus at Colonus*.

 – Tulach Alainn – literally, 'Beautiful Height', translated by Owen and Yolland as 'Fair Hill'.

24 Ennis – a town in County Clare.

 – Kerry – a county in the south of Ireland.

25 Euripides – (480–406 BC) Greek dramatist.

26 the old man – patriarch of the family; it is not a disrespectful term.

27 poteen – whiskey made from potatoes, pronounced 'potcheen'. It is very strong.

28 taking a hand – making fun.

 – Omagh – the main town of County Tyrone.

32 aqua vitae – 'water of life', whiskey.
33 triangulation – measurement of land by a network
  of triangles calculated by trigonometry.
 – hydrographic – surveying and mapping of flowing
  and navigable water.
 – topographic – describing or representing the
  features of a particular place.
35 Hibernophile – lover of Ireland and all things Irish.
45 Ceann Balor – Balor's Head (Balor was an Irish
  king); Lis Maol – Maol's Fort; Baile na gGall –
  Foreigner's Town; Carraig na Ri – King's Rock;
  Mullach Dearg – Red Summit.
46 Loch an Iubhair – Lake of the Yew.
  capped – stopped.
47 East India Company – a trading company
  established in 1600 in the East Indies to enable trade
  between England and Asia.
 – Tra Bhan – White Strand.
  Battle of Waterloo – (1815) British forces led by the
  Duke of Wellington (1769–1852) defeated
  Napoleon I (1769–1821).
 – Bastille – the Paris prison destroyed during the
  French Revolution.
  [This means Yolland's father is forty-four. In the
  stage-directions Friel indicates that Yolland is in his
  late twenties/early thirties, which is inconsistent
  with this information. It might be better to consider
  Yolland as a younger man in his early twenties.
  Certainly this would be more in keeping with his
  behaviour and his friendship with Owen.]
  Apocalypse – signifying a new beginning.
48 Apollo – son of Zeus.
 – Cuchulainn and Ferdia – heroic figures in ancient

Irish sagas. Cuchulainn was known as the Hound of Ulster.

49 Ovid – (43 BC–AD 18) Latin poet.

– William Wordsworth – (1770–1850) English poet.

51 The Pentaglot Preceptor – literally, Five Language Teacher.

71 Mayo – county in the west of Ireland.

– Julius Caesar – (c. 101–44 BC) Roman general and writer.

– Aeschylus – (525–456 BC) founder of Greek tragic drama.

74 Visigoths, Huns, Vandals – three tribes known for their marauding armies.

– Thermopylae – a pass in eastern Greece between mountains and the sea, site of a famous battle between the Spartans and the Persians in 480 BC.

85 Cork – county and city in the south of Ireland.

Making History

The Play

With *Making History*, Friel reaches even farther back into Irish history for his source, to the point in 1603 where Hugh O'Neill, Earl of Tyrone, attempted to forge a coalition between Ireland and Spain in order to drive Elizabeth's English forces out of Ulster. The play covers wide-ranging public events, which are charted by Friel in a series of scenes between O'Neill and his wife and intimates, rendered in a lively contemporary idiom. Friel, who defines the play as 'a dramatic fiction', is interested in the process of history and how the 'facts' will be interpreted. O'Neill's 'last battle' is fought in exile as a dialectic between him and Archbishop Lombard, the Primate of All Ireland, who is writing the 'official' version of O'Neill's life. O'Neill argues passionately that his 'history' should incorporate all his failures and not mythologise the truth. Lombard counters: 'I am offering Gaelic Ireland two things. I'm offering them this narrative that has the elements of myth. And I'm offering them Hugh O'Neill as a national hero. A hero and the story of a hero' (p. 88). In *Making History*, Friel shows a life being 'translated' into myth. It could be perceived that O'Neill has not 'made history'; rather, *it* has used *him*.

The figure of the charismatic but doomed O'Neill also offers Friel the opportunity to develop further previously explored themes. O'Neill was fostered by both the Irish and the English aristocracy, hence his sense of duality. His particular dilemma as the product of two apparently irreconcilable cultures, and the burden he bears as leader of his people, provides a fascinating insight into the relationship between O'Neill's public and private self. And O'Neill's marriage to the impressive Mabel Bagenal – an inspired choice of partner – shows once again the problems that beset those who attempt to embrace 'the other' by crossing tribal and cultural boundaries. Hugh O'Neill has rare qualities, but first and foremost he wants to be judged by history as an ordinary man. Lombard, however, has the final word: 'A man, glorious, pure, faithful above all / Who will cause mournful weeping in every territory. / He will be a God-like prince / And he will be king for the span of his life.' (p. 93).

Friel used as his source Sean O'Faolain's celebrated *The Great O'Neill*, which was published in 1942 when Friel was thirteen. At the end of his Preface, O'Faolain concludes: 'a talented dramatist might write an informative, entertaining, ironical play on the theme of the living man, helplessly watching his translation into a star in the face of all the facts that had reduced him to poverty, exile and defeat.' Friel was to achieve this with *Making History*, which premièred at the Guildhall in Derry in September 1988.

Historical Context

The historical background to this play is obviously of considerable importance. I have assembled the basic facts leading up to the period of O'Neill's rise and fall. All the information here is referred to at some point in the play.

The Celts were an Indo-European group called 'Keltoi'

by the Greeks and 'Galli' by the Romans. They spread from central Europe into Italy and Spain and west through France and Britain to Ireland. Their arrival appears to have been peaceful and the process of settlement that followed over the next few hundred years resulted in the establishment of the Celtic language and culture in Ireland by 500 BC. The island was divided up into about a hundred small kingdoms, each with their own king. The kingdoms were grouped into five provinces – Ulster, Meath, Leinster, Munster and Connacht. Theoretically all five provinces were ruled by the High King from his throne on the Hill of Tara, although one figure rarely emerged undisputed to assume this title.

After the collapse of the Roman Empire, Ireland assumed an important position at the forefront of Christianity in Europe – the Christianisation of the country having started as early as the fourth century. At around this time also, the people of Ireland adopted for themselves the name 'Goidil' – Gaels – from the Welsh 'Gwyddyl'. The Christian leaders were shrewd in using the tribal nature and scattered settlements of Gaelic society to set up monastic developments, the remote sitings of which were also suited to the inhospitable terrain of the country. Viking raids towards the end of the eighth century culminated in full-scale invasion in the tenth, resulting in the founding of walled cities at the mouths of rivers such as Dublin and Cork. Irish resistance to complete Danish rule was successfully led by the High King Brian Boru at the Battle of Clontarf in 1014. The Vikings that remained integrated with the Irish population but, due to the death of Brian Boru in the battle, Ireland was never unified into one strong kingdom.

The Norman conquest of England in 1066 was followed

a century later by the first Anglo-Norman to cross the Irish sea, the adventurer Richard FitzGilbert de Clare, also known as Strongbow, whose help was sought by the exiled king of Leinster. But Henry II of England was concerned that Strongbow might establish a power-base in Ireland and decided to oversee the situation himself, supported by the only English pope in history, Adrian IV, who gave him authority over all – Irish, Norse and Anglo-Norman. In 1172, Henry II's power was reaffirmed by the next pope, Alexander III, but the native Irish offered spirited resistance and English authority beyond 'the Pale' – an area surrounding Dublin – was ineffective. However, the Anglo-Norman settlers began to integrate with the native Irish to such an extent that in 1366 the Crown introduced the Statutes of Kilkenny, a legislation that prohibited intermarriage, prevented the Irish from entering the walled cities and forbade the English to adopt Irish names, customs or language. Despite these strictures, the Gaelic influence strengthened and, by the end of the fifteenth century, 'the Pale' was reduced to a strip of land immediately around Dublin.

The Fitzgeralds of Kildare emerged as the most powerful Anglo-Norman family in Ireland. The English were preoccupied at home with the War of the Roses and it was to their advantage to let the Fitzgeralds 'rule' rather than installing a deputy with an expensive military force. The Fitzgeralds' authority was concentrated mainly in the east and south-east of the country but was sufficiently effective during the early part of the Tudors' reign. However, Henry VIII's break with Rome changed the situation. The Catholic clergy began to preach rebellion against the Crown and Henry, enriched by the dissolution of the Church in England, was able to reward his supporters.

The Fitzgeralds tried to enlist the Pope to their cause but Henry, who retaliated with aggression, forced them to submit to the Crown. He introduced the Act of Supremacy, making him head of the Church, which the Dublin parliament was obliged through legislation to accept. As a result, three distinct factions emerged: the 'Old English', who were loyal to the King but refused to accept his spiritual supremacy; the Catholic Gaelic Irish; and the 'New English' or 'Upstarts', who had benefited from Henry's gifts of Church property. Henry confiscated the Irish nobles' and chieftains' land, returning it to them to regulate as landlords. His policy was to rule Ireland through Irish 'deputies' loyal to the Crown, as cheaply as possible and without the threat of foreign intervention. However, after his death the authority of the English Crown was challenged again.

Queen Elizabeth I aimed to establish an English colony in Ireland. Elizabeth adopted the policy of 'plantation'. In the 1570s an attempt was made to 'plant' north-east Ulster, the most Gaelic area of the country. Three rebellions ensued. Two led by the Desmonds of Munster were easily quelled, their lands confiscated and given to English settlers, but the third, led by Hugh O'Neill, was more serious. O'Neill had grown up in Elizabeth's court and, as her protégé, was groomed to become Chief of Ulster. He even participated with English forces in crushing the Desmonds. But it gradually became evident to O'Neill that rather than assuming the role of an autonomous Gaelic chieftain he was becoming a pawn of English Protestantism, and he turned against the Queen. O'Neill won a major victory at the battle of Yellow Ford in 1598 but was defeated by the English three years later at the Battle of Kinsale. This last was significant in that O'Neill had secured the support of Spain – the English always feared Irish alliances with their Catholic neighbours, the Spanish and the French. However, in this particular case the Irish and Spanish forces failed to meet each other in time to prove effective against the more professional English army. O'Neill signed the Treaty of Mellifont in 1603. Half a million acres of land were confiscated from the rebellious Irish and 'planted' with English and Irish settlers. The Irish chiefs were still nominally landlords but, denied any real authority, many of them, including O'Neill, preferred exile. Their mass departure to continental Europe in 1607 became known as the Flight of the Earls.

James VI of Scotland succeeded Elizabeth, uniting the two countries. His accession also saw a marked change in the character of Ulster as he encouraged Scots loyal to the Crown to emigrate the short distance across the sea to where newly confiscated land awaited further 'plantation'. The Plantation of Ulster offered a way of attaining power over the rebellious region without the expense to the Government of maintaining a large garrison. The planted settlements became Protestant sentinels, standing out as bastions of Anglo-Scottish rule in Ulster. By 1641 there were somewhere between fifty and a hundred thousand English and Scottish settlers 'planted' in Ulster. There was little intermarriage with the planters so the whole country, and Ulster in particular, became divided along Catholic and Protestant lines.

The Irish c. 1600

Francisco de Cuellar was a member of the Spanish Armada of 1588 and was washed up on the Sligo coast. He wandered around the Sligo-Leitrim area for several months and when he finally escaped to Antwerp the following year he wrote up his experiences. His account is interesting in that it gives us the reaction of an aristocratic outsider to the Irish of that time. Much of the information included here is to be found in some form in the play and thus illuminates certain aspects of the text; for example, the position of the clergy, the Gaelic aristocracy's relationship with the Crown, and O'Donnell's mother's imaginative use of debris from the Armada ships.

Going along thus, lost with much uncertainty and toil, I met by chance a clergyman in secular clothing (for the priests go about in that way so that the English may not recognise them) ... He directed me to a castle, six leagues from there. It was very well fortified and belonged to a savage gentleman, a very brave soldier and a great enemy of the Queen of England. He refused to obey her or pay her dues and attended only to his castle ... They carry on perpetual war with the English who keep garrisons for the Queen here. They defend themselves against these English and do not let them enter their territory ... The chief inclination of these people is to be robbers and to plunder each other so that no day passes without a call to arms among them. As soon as one group learns that another group has a large herd of cattle or other animals, they immediately come armed in the night and attack and kill their neighbours. Then the English in the garrisons, learning of this raid, attack the marauders and take all the plunder away from them. The Irish, then, have no other remedy but to withdraw themselves to the mountains with their women and their cattle; for they possess no other property or moveables or clothing ...

These Irish savages liked us well because they knew we had come to attack the English heretics who were such great enemies of theirs. Indeed, had it not been for these savages who guarded us as they would themselves, we would all have been murdered. And for this we were grateful. At the same time these Irish were the first to rob us and strip us to the skins when we were washed ashore. And they obtained great riches in jewellery and money from the bodies of those aristocratic members of the 13 Armada ships which sank with their full crews along those coasts ... (From Captain Cuellar's *Narrative*, reprinted in the programme of the Field Day production, 1988)

Dramatic Narrative

The play uses actual and imagined events from O'Neill's life. For example, Friel extends Mabel's life by ten years and presents us with a Hugh O'Donnell half the age of the original. Friel explains that 'when there was a tension between historical "fact" and the imperative of fiction, I'm glad to say I kept faith with the narrative' (Friel's programme note for Field Day's première production). To clarify the narrative I have outlined here the main events covered in the play either as part of the stage-action or by report:

– O'Neill marries Mabel Bagenal, one of the New English, a Protestant. She is twenty, twenty-one years younger than O'Neill and his third wife. Sir Henry Bagenal, her brother, is the Queen's Marshal. He accuses O'Neill of bigamy regarding former marriages and threatens to bring a charge of abduction in respect of his marriage to Mabel

(p. 7). Mary, her sister, visits Dungannon to persuade her
to return to the family home in Newry (pp. 26–39).

– England attempts to isolate Ulster from the south by
building new fortifications from Dundalk to Sligo. In
addition, existing forts such as Newry (Sir Henry
Bagenal's home) are to be strengthened. Tribal squabbling
within the Gaelic constituency continues (pp. 4–5, 12–13),
and O'Neill is obliged to sustain a delicate balance
between supporting his fellow chieftains and a semblance
of loyalty to the Crown (pp. 35–8).

– Philip II of Spain offers assistance to O'Neill on the
understanding that O'Neill is defending the Catholic
cause against the English. Lombard believes that Europe
is looking to Ireland 'as the ideal springboard for the
Counter-Reformation' (p. 12). However, the Archbishop's
contact in the Spanish court, the Duke of Lerma, perceives
the Gaelic domain fragmented by warring tribes.
Lombard maintains that 'if we can forge ourselves into
a cohesive unit' and convince the Spanish that the Irish are
'a united people' then the help will be forthcoming (p. 15).
The promise of support is eventually formalised by the
Spanish Council of State and endorsed by the King.
O'Neill, now with a price on his head, decides to spear-
head the uprising and plans the campaign (pp. 47–50).
Mabel opposes O'Neill's decision but he persists (pp. 50–
5). Mabel reveals that she is pregnant. News comes that
the Spanish Army will land at Kinsale, a port in the south
of the country far from O'Neill's potential forces.

– The Battle of Kinsale is a disaster, lasting less than an
hour. The uprising collapses with only a small number of
Gaelic chieftains still offering resistance. The majority of
tribes scatter in disarray and Mountjoy, the new Lord
Deputy, controls the country. O'Neill and his followers

hide in the Sperrin Mountains. O'Neill's lands are confiscated and Mountjoy smashes the O'Neill crowning stone at Tullyhogue. O'Donnell hands over Tyrconnell to his brother Rory and intends to go into exile (pp. 62–3). Encouraged by Mabel, O'Neill prepares his submission to the Queen. Mabel goes to her kinsmen to await the birth of the baby. Harry brings news that Mabel and the baby boy have died. Lombard moves to Rome (pp. 69–71).
– O'Neill is exiled in Rome where he lives in punury with Catriona, his fourth wife, and Harry. O'Donnell is dead. Lombard is writing O'Neill's 'history' (pp. 71–93).

The Stage-World

Locale

The play has three different locations – two in Ireland and one in Italy. Act One is situated in Dungannon, County Tyrone, from where the O'Neills ruled Ulster for over five centuries. Nearby is Tullyhogue Fort, the site of the inaugural ceremonies of the O'Neills, where chiefs were crowned from the twelfth to the seventeenth centuries, and it was in Tullyhogue forest that O'Neill tribesmen hid after the Flight of the Earls. However, there are innumerable references to other places in Ireland, England and continental Europe which take the context of the play well beyond the parochial. There is talk of the new Trinity College in Dublin, the Annual Festival of Harpers in Roscommon, Mellifont Abbey and salmon fishing on the Boyne, horse swimming at Lough Owel, O'Donnell's mother's house in Ballyshannon, the Cistercian monastery at Newry, and sheep-stealing in Killybegs; Essex is incarcerated in the Tower of London, the Freelys have returned to Cornwall, and Mary owns horses from Wales; Lombard comes bearing gifts from the Pope, O'Donnell talks of wine from Bordeaux and Genoa, and so on.

Hugh O'Donnell is Earl of Tryconnell, the old name for County Donegal. O'Donnell tells of 'the shit O'Doherty up in Inishowen' who has been stealing his sheep and exporting them to France (p. 13); and O'Rourke, who is 'threatening to quarter' him, got his comeuppance while away at a funeral in Clare (p. 13). These tales are told with great gusto and a deal of humour but the constant quarrelling is symptomatic of the unruly tribal squabbles which have existed for centuries. O'Donnell also graphically illustrates – by tearing a piece of paper in two and then into quarters – how the English are planning to separate him and O'Neill from the south and each other, and, once they are safely isolated, move in on both of them (p. 12). The areas controlled by the Gaelic chiefs are in close proximity to those 'planted' by the English, but the communities are vastly different in character. Mabel has eloped from Newry, which is only fifty miles away, but she is disorientated: 'Everything's so different here. I knew it would be strange – I knew that. But I didn't think it would be so ... foreign ... I feel very far away from everything I know' (p. 25).

Act Two, Scene One, is set somewhere near the Sperrin Mountains. These cover a huge area and reach well over 2,000 feet at their highest. Even today they are wild and empty. O'Neill and his followers, including the pregnant Mabel, have been on the run in this inhospitable landscape for many months. O'Donnell paints a vivid picture of the suffering that surrounds them: 'Everywhere you go there are people scavenging in the fields, hoking up bits of roots, eating fistfuls of watercress. They look like skeletons.' O'Donnell quotes his mother, who describes the country in a state of 'complete collapse ... The countryside's in chaos, she says: slaughter, famine, disease. There must be eight thousand people crowded into Donegal Town looking for food' (p. 59). Ulster has been carved up by the English and Mountjoy's 'riding up and down the country and beheading everything that stirs' (p. 59). Kinsale, the site of the débâcle which followed the Spanish landing, is miles away in the south of the island.

Act Two, Scene Two, moves to Rome. The main point about the locality is that it is O'Neill's place of exile where he is tolerated by the Papacy and receives pensions from both Italy and Spain. He meets with his fellow countrymen – Plunkett and O Domhnaill, both in an advanced state of physical deterioration – to discuss their master plan 'to raise an army and retake Ireland'. O'Neill's vision of their glorious return in which he 'will lead the liberating host' is a superb reductive device in which critical distance is achieved through irony and absurd humour.

Setting

All the settings take into account the need for period detail. This would include furniture, dress and properties. An imaginative approximation capturing the spirit of the period is often more exciting than uninspired authenticity, and would work well with Friel's lively, modern linguistic idiom.

In Act One, Scene One, we are once again, as with *Philadelphia* and *Translations*, faced with a '*comfortless room*'. It is '*spacious*' but '*scantily furnished*' and there has been '*no attempt at decoration*' – baronial but bleak.

The flowers are Hugh's attempt to make the place more welcoming. But, unlike the two previous plays, Act One, Scene Two, shows the room transformed by 'a woman's hand'. Mabel *'has added to the furnishings and the room is now comfortable and colourful'*. She is seen *'sitting alone doing delicate and complicated lacework'*. This visual image of femininity and delicacy is tellingly juxtaposed with the auditory image offstage of the *'terrifying sound of a young girl shrieking'* followed by *'boisterous laughter, shouting, horseplay and a rapid exchange in Irish between a young girl and a young man'* (p. 26). Mabel's response is powerfully physicalised as her terror swiftly turns to anger and she furiously shouts her rebuke. Aspects of the two cultures are sharply contrasted here in these few brief moments.

Act Two, Scene One, is basically an earthbound open space where the location is suggested through the state of the characters' clothes, the nature of the props they carry – leather bags, wooden boxes, water bottles, etc. – and lighting and sound to create the appropriate ambience and atmosphere. It is cold, wet and miserable.

Act Two, Scene Two, in Rome is another *'scantily furnished'* room. Lombard's desk dominates the space. In the centre of the desk is a large book – the history – the visual symbol over which O'Neill's last battle is fought. The room is lit by candlelight and offers the designer an opportunity to create a different ambience and atmosphere to the Irish scene. Caravaggio's paintings might be a suitable visual point of reference. The candlelight will fill the space with shadows – a suitable setting for 'a haunting', for the room is full of ghosts from O'Neill's past and he is tormented by failure.

Friel only mentions costume with regard to specific

items of dress; for example, O'Neill's dandified jacket in the first scene made in London for his wedding celebrations. It is not described – we only know its colour is not maroon (p. 3). Harry recalls Mabel's 'blue dress with a white lace collar and white lace cuffs' that she wore on her twentieth birthday when he and Hugh first met her (p. 71), but whether or not the audience see her in this is a design decision. Although not specifically alluded to, we should assume that Lombard will be dressed in his working robes of office – a constant reminder of his 'calling', position and authority. One small item of costume has particular significance, however. Towards the end of the first scene Mabel assures O'Neill that she will adjust to her new life in time, and affirms that 'We're a tough breed, the Upstarts.' Then, O'Neill gives Mabel a wedding present – a watch worn on the finger like a ring. Only one other woman has one – the Queen. This tender moment of conjoining, as Mabel accepts the beautiful gift, is consummated by her final words: 'We're a tough breed, the O'Neills' (p. 26).

An emblematic device not referred to by Friel but which might appear in some form in a production is O'Neill's seal. Faber use it as an illustration on the front cover of the published text.

Dramatic Structure

There are two acts divided by the Battle of Kinsale. The four scenes provide the framework for the linear action which takes place over two years (historical time is telescoped for dramatic purposes), and Friel indicates the timescale at the top of each scene. Because all the major events take place offstage, Friel has a considerable amount of information to convey to the audience regarding both historical background and current events. He achieves this feat of exposition in Act One, Scene One, by the means of Harry's report to O'Neill (pp. 1–8), and an interlocking duologue in which O'Donnell tells of local news while Lombard fills in the foreign affairs (pp. 9–16). This last sequence is also character-based – the verbose Earl who never listens; the equally single-minded although more circumspect Archbishop. In Act One, Scene Two, Mary imparts a great deal of information about developments on the Bagenals' estate at Newry and their father's last days. We will consider some of this under another heading below. The interesting structural features of this scene, however, are O'Neill's speeches about Maguire and Bagenal, and the long passage about his time in England. The former is virtually a monologue and the latter, although there are other characters present onstage, is essentially a soliloquy. The scene concludes with a debate between O'Neill and Mabel about the wisdom of his actions. Mabel's case is a strong one and, as he admits later, the right one (pp. 50–54). We will return to the substance of this scene in a later section.

In Act Two, Scene One, the exposition is again provided by O'Donnell, giving details of the aftermath of Kinsale, and Harry, who provides a moving account of Mabel's death. Friel splits the recital of O'Neill's submission to the Queen between O'Donnell (reading) and O'Neill (speaking by heart) to show their varying responses. Note how O'Donnell changes his attitude as the gravity of the situation slowly dawns on him (pp. 64–7). O'Neill's tone foreshadows the reprise of the submission in the closing moments of the play when we see him a completely broken man. The exposition in Act Two, Scene Two, is conveyed through O'Neill's conversation with Harry, but the major part of the scene is presented as a dialectic between O'Neill and Lombard, as each presents his version of the 'truth' of O'Neill's story.

Language

Making History's sixteenth-century context is expressed in the language of today. Thus the story and argument are entirely accessible to a modern audience. Friel presents us with a play about history, not a 'history play'. However, status, lineage and origin are defined by different kinds of language, dialect and accent. It is important to remember that O'Neill speaks with an upper-class English accent – 'like those old English nobs in Dublin' (p. 23) – except when he resorts to an Irish brogue as indicated by Friel in the text. At these pertinent moments O'Neill is making a specific point about himself and his national, tribal and cultural roots. Mabel and Mary speak with a trace of Staffordshire accent. Harry is 'Old English' and Lombard is Primate of all Ireland, both educated and cultured men, a fact reflected in their language. O'Donnell has a strong Irish brogue, presumably with a Donegal accent – Mabel says 'he speaks so funny' – and his more colloquial language reflects his boisterous character and more provincial background. As with all Friel's plays each character has his or her own distinctive speech-patterns and idiosyncratic words or phrases.

Metaphor

The text sustains a complex web of metaphor relating to race, culture and identity. Friel highlights the central notions of pasture and husbandry in the discussion

between Mary and Mabel. We know that the Gaelic
landowners have large herds of livestock from O'Donnell's
references to the rustling that goes on between the tribes,
and from Mabel's astonishment at the number of cows and
horses she can see from her bedroom window when she
first arrives at O'Neill's house, 'millions of them stretching
away to the hills' (p. 22). In Act One, Scene Two, however,
we learn that the New English, or Upstarts, have made
very different use of the land. Mary tells her sister of the
developments to their estate: over a hundred hives and
four thousand pounds of honey; the four orchards of a
thousand trees – apple, plum, damson, pear – planted on
bogland which had been drained, ploughed and fenced; the
'great success' of the herb garden sown in the 'little square
where we used to have the see-saw'; in fact every piece of
arable land used to its full potential. Mary has brought
with her boxes of nectarine and quince, jars of honey and a
selection of herb seeds. In response to Mary's apparently
innocent questions about orchards and vegetable-growing
on the Gaelic estates, Mabel says defensively, 'We go in for
pastoral farming – not husbandry; cattle, sheep, horses.
We have two hundred thousand head of cattle here at the
moment – as you have heard.' She deflects any further
discussion on this subject by asking about Mary's herb
garden (p. 29).

Mary, prompted by the offstage 'shrieks' and speaking
'with concern and passion', attempts to persuade Mabel
to return home with her. She equates 'pastoral farming'
with 'neglect of the land', denouncing the Gaelic Irish as
uncivilised, 'And a savage people who refuse to cultivate
the land God gave us have no right to that land.' She
accuses the Gaelic Irish of treachery, treason and religious
superstition, and, despite 'their foreign friends and popish

plotting', pronounces them doomed, 'because their way of life is doomed. and they are doomed because civility is God's way ... and because superstition must yield to reason.' Mabel reveals to the appalled Mary that she 'became a Roman Catholic six months ago'. She defends O'Neill and his people: 'As for civility I believe that there is a mode of life here that is at least as honourable and as cultivated as the life I've left behind.' She reminds Mary of the unpalatable truth that their home in Newry was once a monastery for Cistercian monks which had been routed by their grandfather, 'an agent of civilisation' (p. 33); and roundly defends O'Neill's womanising as 'part of his culture' and his vacillating loyalty to the Crown as 'politics' (p. 33).

O'Neill develops the metaphor in his conversation with Mary by contrasting the two cultures in the figures of Maguire, the old dispensation and personification of the Gaelic civilisation, and her brother Henry Bagenal, the new dispensation and personification of the New English culture: 'Impulse, instinct, capricious genius, brilliant improvisation – or calculation, good order, common sense, the cold pragmatism of the Renaissance mind. Or to use a homely image that might engage you: pasture – husbandry.' He acknowledges that Mary also recognises what he knows, that 'the conflict isn't between carica-tured national types but between two deeply opposed civilisations ... We're really talking about a life-in-death conflict ... Only one will survive.' (p. 37)

O'Neill also plays a game with Mary's seeds, putting the appropriate herb with the person according to temperament: 'Coriander Maguire ... Borage O'Donnell'; picking out dill for Harry, who has a 'comforting and soothing effect' (p. 40). Dill and borage, however, have

been mentioned earlier by Mary. Borage 'likes the sun but
it will survive wherever you plant it – it's very tough'; but
dill should never be planted near fennel because 'the two
will cross-fertilise ... You'll end up with a seed that's
neither one thing or the other' (p. 29). Whether or not this
is a conscious allusion by Mary to O'Neill and Mabel's
marriage, the metaphor is clear – hybridisation. It is a
warning against unions of different cultures, races and
religions. It reflects also upon Mary's closed mind; unlike
Mabel and O'Neill, she could never embrace 'the other'. It
is perhaps worth remembering here O'Donnell and
Lombard's initial response to news of the marriage.
O'Donnell tells O'Neill to 'keep her for a month and then
kick her out', and Lombard warns that they 'have all got
to assess the religious and political implications of this
association' (p. 19). Both men eventually take her hand
but neither will speak to her, and Lombard leaves soon
after (p. 22).

The Characters

Each character in *Making History* is defined by their
atttiude towards O'Neill and the consequences of his
actions in his private and public life. Although all the
characters are finely drawn, their interest to the audience
lies mainly in the shades of opinion and argument they
represent in response to O'Neill's deeds and conduct on
the political stage and in the historical moment. Finally,
O'Neill engages in his last battle, with Lombard as his
adversary. We will begin by examining O'Neill's duality,
then consider each character in relation to him as protagonist, and conclude by analysing the duel between
O'Neill and Lombard.

HUGH O'NEILL

I should like to draw your attention first to O'Neill's soliloquy in Act One, Scene Two (pp. 45–7). It comes at a time of tremendous pressure, when he is being hailed as the leader of a holy crusade of the Counter-Reformation at the head of an emergent nation-state united under papal colours. There is an imperative for him to act decisively and assume responsibility. At this most public moment, O'Neill withdraws into himself and remembers his time in England with Sir Henry Sidney and Lady Mary – 'I loved them both very much.' See how he describes his life at Penshurst in Kent – 'a golden and beneficent land' – where he 'was conscious not only that new ideas and concepts were being explored and fashioned but that I was being explored and fashioned at the same time'. He was aware that Sir Henry possessed 'grace and tact' which transformed the 'naked brutality and imperial greed' of such 'gross' and 'vain men' as Drake and Frobisher 'into boyish excitement and manly adventure'.

But there was a sting in the tail, that 'trivial little hurt, that single failure in years of courtesy' which 'has pulsed relentlessly in a corner of my heart'. Sidney's 'disquisition' at the young O'Neill's farewell dinner, before he returned to Ireland 'to become a leader of his people', defined him as 'Fox O'Neill' – 'Those Irishmen who live like subjects play but as the fox which when you have him on a chain will seem tame; but if he ever gets loose, he will be wild again.' Here Sidney points to the heart of O'Neill's dilemma, the duality of his person which he is unable to resolve. The condition is endemic because of O'Neill's peculiar upbringing; fostered by both the English and the Irish, he is the product of two seemingly irreconcilable cultures. However, as O'Neill faces the greatest decision of his life he quietens the pulse of resentment, forgives Sir Henry, and declares his love for the colonist. He also maintains his privacy. In public, the private man prevails.

O'Neill is aware of the burden that he carries. He declares it to Mabel with '*controlled passion*' as she tries to persuade him to abandon the Spanish plan (p. 53). He acknowledges the 'assurances and dignities' of Gaelic culture and honours their 'rituals and ceremonies and beliefs', many of which go back to ancient times and, while retaining them, has tried to 'open these people to the strange new ways of Europe, to ease them into the new assessment of things, to nudge them towards changing evaluations and beliefs'. It is important to recognise O'Neill as a European figure, fluent in several languages, respected by heads of state and wise in the ways of real-politick. In many respects he is a born leader: intelligent, charismatic, responsible and politically astute. He understands both the English and Irish psyche and, because of this, knows that he is between a rock and a hard place: 'Two pursuits that can scarcely be followed simultaneously. Two tasks that are almost self-cancelling. But they have got to be attempted because the formation of nations and civilisations is a willed act, not a product of fate or accident.' He knows also that the slow, sure tide of history is with him and that if he has the patience to sit and wait, the dilemma will be resolved.

O'Neill has presented a similar argument earlier to Mary, in Mabel's presence, only this time personalised in the forms of Maguire, the Fermanagh chieftain, and their brother Sir Henry Bagenal. Which hand should he grasp? 'The Queen Marshal's? ... using Our Henry as a symbol of the new order which every aristocratic instinct in my body disdains but which my intelligence comprehends and indeed grudgingly respects ... or do I grip the hand of the Fermanagh rebel and thereby bear public and imprudent witness to a way of life that my blood comprehends and indeed loves and that is as old as the book of Ruth?' (p. 38). Maguire seeks help from the 'compromised' O'Neills. O'Neill has 'trotted behind the Tudors on several expeditions against the native rebels' (p. 37), but this time he chooses to lead his people with catastrophic results. The perfumed courtier, political tactician, civilised chieftain and leader of the Gaelic Irish becomes a fugitive in his own country. 'Fox O'Neill' has turned wild again and is now on the run. O'Neill's submission to the Queen is masterly in its abject obeisance. He is, however, profoundly ashamed of it. When he finishes reading with O'Donnell there is a long silence and then, '*O'Neill moves away as if to distance himself from what he has just read*' (p. 66).

O'Neill is at his most revealing in the final scene. Here he presents us with a parody of his former self as he describes a day in exile to Harry – 'The usual feverish political activity and intellectual excitement': obsequiously receiving his two pensions from the papal and Spanish authorities; pathetically grateful for the ministrations of the whore Maria; and meeting his fellow exiles, the equally decrepit Gaelic chiefs Plunkett and O Domhnaill, to discuss their master plan to retake Ireland. He is a bitter man full of contempt for his own shortcomings but deeply concerned to tell the truth about his failures and to affirm the centrality of Mabel to his life.

MABEL BAGENAL

Mabel is an exemplary figure. She is described by Friel as '*forthright, determined*' and by O'Neill as 'a very

talented, a very spirited, a very beautiful young woman'
(p. 19); and although 'she's not exactly Helen of Troy'
(p. 7), she has obviously turned O'Neill's head. More
importantly, she is his intellectual equal with a wisdom
beyond her years. Despite her antecedents, she eventually
inspires love in O'Donnell and respect from the archbishop. When we first see her she is nervous at meeting
both these men – 'Butcher O'Donnell' and 'a popish
priest' – and almost believes Hugh when he teasingly tells
her that her hand is turning black. She is in an alien
environment, removed from her own kind and unable to
return to them having betrayed her tribe by eloping with
and marrying – albeit with the sanction of a Protestant
priest – 'the Northern Lucifer'. Mabel's vulnerability is
apparent but so is her courage. It is also important to note
the ease of their intimacy in this early scene (pp. 22–6).

Our sympathy remains with Mabel into the following
scene and is reinforced by her response to the crude
intrusion of the offstage couple (p. 26). She longs for her
sister to stay – 'Please. For my sake. Please' (p. 27) – and is
deeply hurt when she realises that her father, although he
'forgot nobody', left no 'personal messages' for her before
he died (p. 30). Disowned by her father, treated like
property by her brother – 'He still talks about taking you
home by force' – she is, however, greatly missed by Mary.
Their relationship is not without tension, they 'always
fight after a few hours' (p. 27), but there is an ulterior
motive to Mary's visit to Dungannon a year after the
marriage – to take Mabel back with her to the family
home in Newry. The sense of loss is mutual but Mabel
insists, 'This is my home' (p. 32).

But Mabel really comes into her own in her dispute
with O'Neill over his proposed alliance with Spain.

Unlike Harry, Lombard and O'Donnell, she is not privy to O'Neill's soliloquy but returns to the room after he has begun to set the plans in train. She warns him that this is not 'his way' of doing things – every important move he has ever made 'has been pondered for months', and she senses that his instinct now 'is not to gamble everything on one big throw that is more than risky'. She is convinced that Spain is using him: 'England will throw everything she has' into the war but 'It's not Spain's war. It's your war.' She knows that the Gaelic Irish are not united, they have no single leader, describing them 'as an impromptu alliance of squabbling tribesmen' who are 'grabbing at religion as a coagulant only because they have no other idea to inform them or give them cohesion' (p. 51). O'Neill's riposte is to accuse her of thinking like an Upstart, which he immediately regrets – he *grabs her and holds her in his arms* – conceding that she is right. He also reveals his concern for O'Donnell's enthusiasm and confesses that he is never sure what the archbishop is thinking (p. 52).

Mabel is suspicious of Lombard's vision of a Catholic Confederation with O'Neill as the figurehead of a 'glorious Catholic Counter-Reformation', deducing that the archbishop's first consideration is 'Rome and Roman power', just as 'Spain's only interest is in Spain and Spanish power.' Despite Mabel's conversion to Catholicism, this view may be informed by her inculcated Protestantism, but she claims that 'my only real concern is you, Hugh'. She also foresees that 'when the war is over, whatever the outcome, the Lombards and the Oviedos won't be here – they'll have moved on to more promising territories'. Others will be acting out of self-interest whereas Mabel perceives that O'Neill is genuinely attempting to fulfil his role as a leader of his people. She apologises for having spoken, for 'intruding'. Note the three pauses which draw attention to her final statement – 'I'm sure I don't really understand the overall thing' (p. 52). O'Neill repeats the phrase twice, the second time followed by the qualification, 'we don't even begin to know what it means'. There is then a '*Silence*' between them while this idea is absorbed by them and the audience. It is in the context of 'the overall thing' that Mabel and O'Neill's union is of such vital importance. Their relationship is seen to be tough and argumentative but it is based on mutual respect and a genuine desire to understand 'the other', thus overcoming the barriers that have traditionally divided their respective people.

As Mabel prepares to leave the room she breaks her promise to Mary and tells O'Neill about Mountjoy's appointment – her loyalties now lie with her husband. But O'Neill's response is to define the two 'self-cancelling tasks' which he is obliged to pursue. Mabel's rejoinder to his lengthy explanation is a robust rejection of his position: 'So have your war … So go and fight. That's what you've spent your life doing. That's what you're best at. Fighting to preserve a fighting society. I don't care any more.' O'Neill's rebuttal becomes sectarian and persona-lised and, ultimately, abusive (pp. 53–4). Mabel retorts by demanding that O'Neill removes his mistresses from the house – a fact she has been prepared to overlook up to this point – or else she leaves. The argument degenerates further into a domestic row when she reveals that she is pregnant, O'Neill cruelly forcing her to face his profligate talent for siring illegitimate children – 'Or so my people boast. An affectionate tribute every nation bestows on its heroes' (p. 55). He has '*instant remorse*', but any

reconciliation is thwarted by O'Donnell's jubilant inter-
ruption that the date for the Spanish fleet to set sail is 3
September. This is the last we see of Mabel.

However, it is not the last we hear of her. O'Neill's
actions after Kinsale are informed by Mabel's advice. He
confides in O'Donnell that his instinct is to leave Ireland.
Mabel is urging him 'to hang on, pick up the pieces, start
all over again'. He admits that the New English are 'very
tenacious' (p. 63). O'Donnell praises Mabel as a 'very
loyal wee girl'. She advocates that O'Neill should submit
to Elizabeth, who would restore him to his previous
position provided she could rule Ireland through him.
Believing that O'Neill would never betray his people,
Mabel is convinced that those New English who 'are sick
of England' would join with O'Neill and those who have
remained loyal to him, to form a new constituency in
Ireland. Here is the possibility of a fresh start, and new
beginning. O'Donnell concedes that O'Neill is 'a tenacious bugger, too. You and Mabel are well met.' The
potential for a new beginning dies with Mabel and her
baby boy, scarcely an hour old. However, O'Neill returns
to Mabel and the centrality of her place in his history
during his debate with Lombard in the final scene. The
archbishop will consign her to a footnote in his book but
we will share O'Neill's knowledge of the importance of
her contribution to 'the overall thing' and what could
have been.

HUGH O'DONNELL O'Donnell is the antithesis of O'Neill,
portrayed as a hot-headed youth, a bit of a clown, un-
diplomatic and politically naive. But he is an appealing
character and often genuinely funny. Friel describes him
as 'impulsive' and 'enthusiastic' with 'a deep affection' for

O'Neill. He never doubts O'Neill's intentions nor does he see beyond the present. He treats the rebellion like a great adventure – 'cattle-raiding on an international scale' – but is, nevertheless, matured in defeat. Note his generosity towards the family beginning on the roadside near Raphoe, his anger at the possibility that the Irish were betrayed at Kinsale, and his dismay at the resulting chaos he sees around him (pp. 57–60). His decision to resign has not come easily or quickly. He recognises his brother's qualities as well as his own shortcomings: 'Rory'll be a fine chieftain – he's a solid man, very calm, very balanced. He hasn't my style or flair, of course; but then I have a fault or two, as you know. The blood gets up too easy . . .' (p. 62).

O'Donnell, however, epitomises the Irishman's love of the land, which he defines as 'the goddess that every ruler in turn is married to'. He knows that chieftains 'come and go but she stays the same'. With Rory's accession, 'the Tyrconnell goddess is getting a new man. Trouble is, no matter who she's married to, I'll always be in love with her.' On the point of breaking down, he impulsively *flings his arms around O'Neill*. This is characteristic behaviour – his emotions near to the surface and liable to spill over – but his manner has a new gravity. This is even more apparent when reading through O'Neill's submission to the Queen – 'This is the end of it all, Hugh, isn't it?' (p. 67).

THE BAGENALS Sir Henry Bagenal became Queen's Marshal on his father's death. O'Neill points out that 'London couldn't have a more dutiful servant than our Henry . . . it's the plodding Henrys of this world who are the real empire-makers' (p. 36). And in his indignation at

O'Neill's 'treachery' in marrying Mabel, O'Donnell reminds Harry that 'Butcher Bagenal was ... Raiding and plundering with a new troop of soldiers over from Chester – the way you'd blood young greyhounds! Slaughtered and beheaded fifteen families that were out saving hay along the river bank, men, women and children. With the result that ... there are over a hundred refugees in my mother's place in Donegal Town' (pp. 19–20). Henry, although offstage, is a considerable force and an important representative of the Tudor political machine.

Friel portrays Mary as a credible elder sister to Mabel. She is extremely vulnerable as an intelligent young woman within her own culture. Her options are limited and we are shown the bleak prospect of her marriage to 'Young Patrick Barnewall' (p. 31). Mary is 'thinking seriously about it' because 'he's still one of us ... and whatever about his age, he's a man of great honour,' and 'our Henry thinks very highly of him'. In a sense Mary is a victim of her own prejudice, which sees the Gaelic Irish, in effect all Roman Catholics, as outside the law and 'steeped in religious superstition'. We have already discussed this in some detail in the section on metaphor but it is as well to remind ourselves that this and the way O'Neill uses Mary as a butt for his own analysis of the difference between the two cultures, show that she lacks Mabel's vision, imagination and courage. It is important that we see the contrast between the two sisters and, by implication, Mabel and her brother. And, despite Mabel's undoubted love for her father, she has outgrown the whole family's narrow way of thinking.

HARRY HOVEDON The faithful retainer is a representative of the Old English. We only learn of Harry's lineage late on in the play when O'Neill is abusing his loyalty, faith and fealty (p. 79), but Harry's past, including his skill for survival, would be manifest in the character's demeanour and attitude. O'Neill claims that he chose Harry Hovedon as his private secretary 'precisely because he wasn't a Gael', and not, therefore, 'vulnerable to small, tribal pressures ... he would be above that kind of petty venality'. Harry left the Old English, or his family 'threw him out' (p. 89), and he embraced O'Neill and the whole Gaelic nation. Whatever Harry's journey might have been he finally 'dedicated' his life to O'Neill (p. 89).

In the first half of the play we see that Harry is responsible for the smooth running of O'Neill's life and is, in some ways, his confidante. He is a born administrator, clear-sighted, prudent and entirely trustworthy. In the final scene O'Neill, angered by what he has read of Lombard's 'history' and refused credit by the wine merchant, accuses Harry of everything of which he is *not* guilty and puts the boot in by adding that 'certainly Mabel was not taken in by it' (p. 79). This is palpably untrue as the relationship between Mabel and Harry appeared to be one of trust and we remember his grief at her death (pp. 70–1). Harry, while maintaining his own dignity, shows us how low Hugh has sunk: 'I'm sorry for you, Hugh. You have become a pitiable, bitter bastard' (p. 79). Because Harry has been presented as a sympathetic character throughout the play we believe his assessment. Because Harry does so, we are also prepared to indulge O'Neill for a little longer.

We recognise, as does Harry, O'Neill's self-loathing and contempt for what he has become. O'Neill uses Harry to articulate his own sourness, bitterness, deep disappointment and the 'corroding sense of betrayal' that is gnawing away at him. O'Neill beats Harry like a dog in an attempt to ease his own pain. Later, in his conversation with Lombard, O'Neill regrets, as he always does, that he was 'cruel to Harry just now'. He goes on: 'I told him Mabel didn't trust him. That was a damned lie. Mabel loved Harry' (p. 81). Before the play ends Harry exchanges an old pair of his shoes – which he claims he did not want – for a bottle of cheap Chianti for O'Neill. Faithful to the end.

PETER LOMBARD Lombard is O'Neill's contemporary and final adversary. Friel defines him as a church diplomat with a 'careful' and 'exact' manner. He is urbane, *'a man of humour and perception and by no means diminished by his profession'* (p. 8). Friel's description is telling because it also defines Friel's attitude towards the public role and function of the archbishop. It is important to remember that the Catholic priesthood was, of necessity, a clandestine constituency. Lombard reminds O'Neill that the members of his priests' network 'have a price on their head, too' (p. 49). Lombard is very involved in the intense diplomacy which precedes the campaign, but appears to draw the line at securing the Excommunication Bull, deeming it a spiritual matter (p. 49). However, Mabel is right to be suspicious of Lombard's motives. When Kinsale proves to be a rout, Lombard leaves for Europe, and O'Donnell wryly observes: 'They don't miss a beat, those boys, do they?' (p. 69). Lombard refers to himself as 'some kind of a half priest, half schemer' (p. 88). O'Neill says that he never quite knows what the archbishop is thinking and this is a useful pointer to the way Lombard conducts himself. He does not show his full hand until the very last moment, by which time it is too late – O'Neill has lost all vestiges of power and influence.

We first hear that Lombard is writing a book on O'Neill from Harry. O'Neill is *'suddenly alert'*, and points out that 'We have our own annalist' (p. 6). O'Neill does not 'like this idea at all' and confronts Lombard soon after (pp. 10–11). Lombard talks about arranging material 'into a shape'; Hugh is concerned about 'the truth', a point he never deviates from throughout the play. Lombard maintains that maybe truth and falsity are not 'the proper criteria'; it may be that 'when the time comes my first responsibility will be to tell the best possible narrative'. He sees history as 'a kind of story-telling', where apparently arbitrary events are shaped into a narrative 'that is logical and interesting'. He claims that 'imagination will be as important as information' and that, therefore, 'truth' 'is not the primary ingredient'. Moreover, 'History has to be made – before it's remade' (p. 12). There is a further short exchange immediately after Mabel has been introduced to Lombard and O'Donnell. Here Lombard introduces the idea that he is not altogether his own man: 'To an extent I simply fulfil the needs, satisfy the expectations' (p. 21).

Once O'Neill is in Rome, Lombard becomes a fixture in the household and, although Lombard protests that he only has 'an outline', the work is clearly far advanced. In their late-night conversation the battle lines are soon drawn. Hugh does not trust Lombard to tell the truth. Lombard, who has assessed *'the situation instantly and accurately'* when he happens on the row between O'Neill and Harry, tries a little psychological manipulation. On the question of O'Neill's wives he says, '(*confidentially*) But I've got to confess a secret unease, Hugh ... the fact that O'Neill had four, shall we say acknowledged, wives, do you think that may strike future readers as perhaps ...

a surfeit? I'm sure not. I'm sure I'm being too sensitive. Anyhow we can't deliberately suppress what we know did happen, can we?' (p. 82). Lombard knows that Hugh is maudlin and vulnerable and uses all his diplomatic tact and cunning to slowly wear him down.

Physically contrasted – O'Neill slumped sulkily in a chair; Lombard spry and energised, relishing his drink – and visually inhabiting their own space onstage, the two men engage. They continue to use Christian names but the struggle over the life of Hugh O'Neill is played out to the death. Each point made by Lombard is countered by O'Neill. To briefly summarise the thrust of Lombard's 'history': he cites O'Neill's birth, 'noble genealogy' and the formative years that he spent fostered with the O'Quinns and the O'Hagans; moves on to the years of consolidation of O'Neill's 'position as the pre-eminent Gaelic ruler in the country' and his 'early intimations ... of an emerging nation state'; then isolates three key moments: when Hugh was proclaimed The O'Neill at Tullyhogue, marking six hundred and thirty years of O'Neill hegemony; the Nine Years War and the 'legendary' Battle of Kinsale and 'the crushing of the most magnificent Gaelic army ever assembled'; finally, 'The Flight of the Earls', as he coins it, 'That tragic but magnificent exodus of the Gaelic aristocracy' (p. 86).

O'Neill intercuts with the following omissions and rejoinders: he spent nine years in England with Leicester and Sidney; his crowning was 'a political ploy ... the very next month I begged Elizabeth for pardon'; the Gaelic Irish were routed by Mountjoy at Kinsale, 'We ran away like rats ... We disgraced ourselves at Kinsale'; and to the romantic notion of 'The Flight of the Earls', O'Neill responds, 'As we pulled out from Rathmullan the

McSwineys stoned us from the shore!' (p. 86). O'Neill reveals that after Kinsale he was obliged to live like a criminal exile in his own country, 'hiding from the English, from the Upstarts, from the Old English, but most assiduously hiding from my brother Gaels who couldn't wait to strip me of every blade of grass I ever owned' (p. 87). When he could no longer bear the humiliation he fled into exile. 'The Flight of the Earls – you make it sound like a lap of honour. We ran away just as we ran away at Kinsale. We were going to look after our own skins! That's why we "took boat" from Rathmullan! That's why the great O'Neill is here – at rest – here in Rome. Because we ran away.' (p. 87).

O'Neill is terrified of being 'embalmed' 'in a florid lie ... in pieties'. He wants it all in: 'The schemer, the leader, the liar, the statesman, the lecher, the patriot, the drunk, the soured, bitter émigré ...' (p. 83). But what *is* the truth? Lombard cites O'Cleary's portrayal of O'Donnell as 'A dove in meekness' – this is not a lie, 'merely a convention' (p. 85) – and he 'proves' Harry could be perceived as a 'traitor' rather than 'a most faithful friend' (p. 89). Lombard, despite frequent offers to rewrite his outline in any way O'Neill wants, is adamant about what he is trying to do: 'People think they just want to know the "facts"; they think they believe in some sort of empirical truth, but what they really want is a story,' which entails 'making a pattern ... offering a cohesion to that random catalogue of deliberate achievement and sheer accident' that constitutes O'Neill's life. He cites the methods of the Four Evangelists when writing the Gospels and asks O'Neill to think of his book 'as an act of pietas'. Lombard is convinced that what Gaelic Ireland and 'a colonised people on the brink of extinction' need now is a myth and a national hero: 'there are times when a hero can be as important to a people as a God. And isn't God – or so I excuse my perfidy – isn't God the perfect hero?' (p. 88).

O'Neill's final rally is made on behalf of his beloved Mabel. Lombard's evasion is met with O'Neill's rage (p. 89). Eventually, in response to O'Neill's persistence as to 'How-will-Mabel-be-portrayed?', Lombard diminishes Mabel's status to a character in a domestic love-story, concluding: 'in the overall thing ... how many heroes can one history accommodate?' (p. 91). He adds, self-deprecatingly: 'And how will I emerge myself for Heaven's sake? At best a character in a subplot. And isn't that adequate for minor people like us?' Mabel, who O'Neill believes to be central to his life, is reduced to one of the 'minor people' in Lombard's 'history'. As Lombard moves to his desk to begin his first public recitation of the 'history', he pauses by O'Neill's chair and says '(*privately*) Trust it, Hugh. Trust it.' The play closes with a recital of Lombard's 'history', counterpointed by O'Neill's shaming submission to Elizabeth. Celebration is juxtaposed with contrition – Lombard loud and confident, O'Neill speaking in a whisper, his Tyrone accent gradually reasserting itself (p. 92). O'Neill's final words of apology and plea for forgiveness are addressed to his wife. He has betrayed both his people and her. By the end, the Great O'Neill is crying.

Endnote

O'Neill wants to be judged as an ordinary man but Lombard creates a narrative designed to elevate him to heroic status for the benefit of future Irish generations.

Lombard's partial story excludes Mabel from 'the overall thing'. O'Neill is vanquished, his last battle ends in total defeat. History has been re-made.

Textual Notes

2 Virgil – (70–19 BC) Roman epic poet who wrote the *Aeneid*.

– Trinity College – now the University of Dublin. Celebrated graduates include the dramatists J. M. Synge and Samuel Beckett.

3 Boyne River – famous in Irish history for the Battle of the Boyne where William, Prince of Orange (William III), defeated James II of England, thus establishing the Protestant Ascendancy in Ireland. 'King Billy', heroically astride a white mare, riding across the Boyne, has become the symbol of Irish Protestants.

4 Brehon Law – the law common to all of the Gaelic tribes.

5 Queen Elizabeth I – (1533–1603) politically and intellectually able, although personally vain and capricious. Her long reign was one of stability, victory over the Spanish, and adventure in the New World; the Church of England was established, and literary work flourished. She executed those who opposed her, including Essex (below) and Mary, Queen of Scots.

– Robert Devereux, Earl of Essex – (1566–1601) a favourite of Queen Elizabeth but proved an unsuccessful Governor General of Ireland. He returned to England against the Queen's wishes, plotted and was executed.

9 bugger – so-and-so; a colloquial term of abuse, here tinged with affection.

10 Philip II of Spain – (1527–98) married Mary Tudor of England, and after her death sent the ill-fated Armada against Elizabeth in 1588.

13 O'Rourke – the family styled themselves Lords of Breffny and ruled territory in Cavan and Leitrim, where their stronghold was at Dromahair on Lough Gill.

– Bordeaux – a seaport in the Gironde area of France famous for its wines and liqueurs.

– Genoa – a city on what is now the Italian Riviera.

14–15 Lombard's thesis – see Historical Context (page 122–4).

17 hoor – whore; the insult 'hoor' can be applied to either men or women.

18 Butcher Bagenal – Sir Henry Bagenal uses the same epithet to describe O'Donnell.

19 jouking – sneaking.

28 Kent – known as the Garden of England.

29 muskets – early type of smooth-bore hand-gun.

38 Robert Dudley, Earl of Leicester – (1538–88) English soldier and favourite of Elizabeth I; commanded forces assembled against the Spanish Armada in 1588.

42 mustering – assembling troops.

44 Dark Rosie – Ireland is known as Dark Rosaleen.

46 Sir Francis Drake – (1540–96) sailed round the world in 1577–80 in the *Golden Hind*. In 1587 he destroyed a number of Spanish ships in Cadiz harbour, and helped to defeat the Spanish Armada in 1588.

– Sir Martin Frobisher – (1534–94) first British

navigator to seek the north-west passage from the Atlantic to the Pacific through the Arctic seas. He also fought against the Spanish Armada.

48 Earl of Argyle – O'Neill is wanting support from Catholic Scotland.

53 Charles Blount, Lord Mountjoy – the Protestant Lord Deputy before whom O'Neill knelt at Mellifont to make his formal submission to the Crown.

62 Bann and Foyle – two of Ireland's main rivers.

70 Edmund Spenser – (1552–99) English poet who went to Ireland in 1580 as the Lord Deputy's secretary, and later acquired Kilcolman Castle, where he wrote most of his main work, *The Fairie Queene*. His castle was burnt in an insurrection in 1598, when he returned to London.

79 fealty – the loyalty of a vassal to his lord.

81 Thucydides – (c.460–399 BC) Greek historian who was not merely a chronicler, but saw the significance of events and tried to give an impartial account.

84 St Patrick – came to Ireland as a sixteen-year-old Roman slave, the victim of Irish pirates who raided a Roman settlement in Britain. He was a natural diplomat and compromiser and as he grew up the Irish kings allowed him to engage in public disputation with the druids. He became accomplished at adapting existing practices and ceremonies to his own mission, and thus Christianity spread peacefully throughout the land.

Dancing at Lughnasa

The Play

In *Dancing at Lughnasa*, Friel returns to Ballybeg, a family drama and memories of childhood. Here Friel draws on his family history and his own experience of false memory. Two of Friel's aunts – 'those five brave Glenties women' to whom the play is dedicated – endured a life of destitution in London after leaving the family home in rural Donegal. As a young man he searched for them, finding the one who survived in a hostel for the homeless and there learnt of their suffering. Friel does not dramatise these events but, more effectively, refers in the narration to the fate of the two aunts in a few simple but powerful sentences that serve to cast a long shadow over the recollections of Michael's summer idyll. Friel has a persistent memory – similar to Gar's in *Philadelphia* – of a day in Glenties spent with his father fishing. He remembers the walk home from the lake in the rain, fishing rods across their shoulders, singing happily until they reach the main street of the town. However, there is no lake on that road and despite the vividness of the memory, what he remembers never actually happened. But Friel remembers it all the same. The memory is 'true' yet untrustworthy. Friel has explored the 'tragic space' between these two notions before, but in the case of *Dancing at Lughnasa* he goes further.

Michael says, 'what fascinates me about memory is that

it owes nothing to fact' (p. 100). In the memory of that summer of 1936 in Ballybeg, 'atmosphere is more real than incident and everything is simultaneously actual and illusory'. The 'atmosphere' is one of 'nostalgia', the literal meaning of which comes from 'nostos' – home – and 'algos' – pain. The historical moment of 1936 at which Friel chooses to set the play is the point where 'The Industrial Revolution had finally caught up with Ballybeg' (p. 83). The precise place is the home of the five Mundy sisters. Agnes and Rose's small income is about to be taken away by the arrival of a knitting factory. Modernisation is replacing the old certainties. As Kate observes, 'suddenly you realise that hair cracks are appearing everywhere; that control is slipping away; that the whole thing is so fragile it can't be held together much longer. It's all about to collapse ...' (p. 50).

The Mundy sisters are experiencing modernisation at the same time as trying to deal with the return of their brother Jack, who, as a missionary in a leper colony in Uganda, ended up espousing the beliefs of the ancient culture he had been sent to convert. The women are dramatically caught between these two worlds. To highlight their dilemma the action of the play occurs at harvest time, when Ballybeg is celebrating the Festival of Lughnasa, where liberated pagan rituals are set against the repressive forces of the Catholic Church. As August gives way to September, the promise of summer is overshadowed by dark forebodings which lead to the break up of the family and a tragic end for two of the sisters. The sisters are such a coherent entity that this fragmentation has tremendous resonance. It is as if the tribe were scattering and losing its identity.

There are elements in the play which touch on

colonisation, cultural domination and the struggle for independence, but Friel's main concern is the conflict outlined above and the human dimension of the tragedy which results from it. He is also intent on creating a theatrical expression which goes beyond language, and there is no doubt that the play's greatest moments are wordless. The magnificent dance sequence early in the first act, in which the sisters abandon themselves to 'Marconi's voodoo', is matchless in its eloquence and vitality, and the genuine excitement it generates. Friel again experiments with form through the device of the narrator, which enables him to move backwards and forwards in time. It provides also a critical distance. Visual images, music and emblematic costumes and props are also utilised to great effect. Comedy and tragedy co-exist: the former executed with a delicate, light touch, the latter experienced at one remove through Michael's narration. He may be taking us back into the past, but there is an emphasis in the stage-action on the present – the Mundy sisters holding on instinctively to whatever joy they can before the world they know slips from their grasp. The sadness which pervades the play is offset by the exhilarating power of 'the dance'. And, of course, although the play explores that space beyond words. Friel still creates language of great power and beauty, particularly in Michael's elegant monologues. His last speech is exquisite.

Historical Context

There are several historical references within the living memory of the Mundy family which it will be helpful to clarify. For example, Uncle Jack was a chaplain to the

British Army in East Africa. His photograph was taken in 1917 during the First World War. But Kate (who would have been born in 1896) had been involved with the Irish war of independence against Britain, 'so Father Jack's brief career in the British army was never referred to in that house' (p. 11). As you know, Ireland's struggle for independence from Britain had been going on for many centuries, but in 1916 an insurrection – known as the Easter Rising – took place in Dublin during which an Irish republic was proclaimed. The Rising, violently suppressed by the British, lasted less than a week and fourteen of the rebellion's leaders were executed. Eamon De Valera, who participated in the Rising, had his sentence commuted – his mother was American – and he went on to lead the political party, Sinn Féin. In 1918, he and his fellow MPs, all of whom refused to sit in the Westminster parliament, set up the Dáil Éireann (Assembly of Ireland). Two years of conflict followed between the Irish Republican Army on the Irish side and the Royal Irish Constabulary and the British Army, reinforced by the Auxiliaries and Black-and-Tans, two quasi-military groups that earned themselves vicious reputations, on the British side. Hostilities were halted by the Government of Ireland Act, which created separate parliaments for 'Northern Ireland' and 'Southern Ireland' (the twenty-six counties of the future Republic including Donegal).

A treaty was negotiated and signed in 1921 which gave 'Southern Ireland', known as the Irish Free State, dominion status within the British Commonwealth. Northern Ireland was perceived as a small entity within the United Kingdom which did not preclude eventual Irish unity. As a result of Partition, the 'immediate and terrible' civil war that Lloyd George, the British Prime Minister, hoped to avoid broke out between those who supported the Treaty (Free Staters) and those who rejected it (die-hard Republicans). De Valera was of the latter faction, but eventually capitulated in 1923, declaring that military victory rested with those who had destroyed the Republic. De Valera abandoned Sinn Féin and formed his own political party in 1926. He chose as its name Fianna Fáil (Soldiers of Destiny) which drew on the symbolism of Ireland's mythical past and conformed with his vision of Ireland as a Celtic Utopia with rural values. De Valera was triumphant in the elections of 1932 and became Taoiseach (prime minister). But the depression of the 1930s was intensified in Ireland due to an economic war with Britain caused by the British Government imposing heavy duties on Irish goods in retaliation for De Valera withholding loan payments. Given the ages of the Mundy sisters, all this would be familiar to them. We do not know to what extent or for how long Kate was involved in nationalist politics but her dislike of the British is evident. De Valera also features in one of Maggie's ditties.

1936 also saw the outbreak of the Spanish Civil War. Gerry joins the International Brigade (p. 31) to support the Popular Front, the incumbent Republican Government, against the Fascist forces of General Franco (p. 50), but is invalided out in Barcelona (p. 61). Gerry's political commitment is questionable, his main claim to involvement seemingly his ability to ride a motorbike. But the play's perspective is broadened by reference to European mass movements – Mussolini, Italy's Fascist dictator, and his Abyssinian adventure, is also mentioned.

Uncle Jack's return from Uganda affords an even wider picture and provides a pertinent example of British colonialism. Jack cites the district commissioner who refuses to speak Swahili and is angered by Jack's refusal to take the money the English give for churches, schools and hospitals (p. 39). He tries to protect Jack from 'going native' by inviting him to Kampala for weekends, but to no avail. Jack has exposed himself totally to the local culture and by so doing feels that he understands the very souls of the people. Friel has Uncle Jack's return to Ireland coincide with the Lughnasa Festival, thus suggesting analogies between the Ryangan harvest ceremonies and those of Celtic Ireland. It is significant that the play was written towards the end of a decade, the 1980s, when 'many priests, nuns and lay missionaries began to return from the Third World imbued with the radical ideas of liberation theology and with the desire to re-establish intellectual and social connections between Ireland and the decolonised world' (Declan Kiberd, *Irish Theatre Magazine*, vol. 1, 3, summer 1999, p. 43). The figure of Uncle Jack, therefore, is particularly important with regard to this debate.

The Lughnasa Festival

In Ireland the harvest festival, held every year in early August, was called Lughnasa after Lugh, the Celtic god, provider of the crops. In 1962, when Maire MacNeill first published her definitive study of *The Festival of Lughnasa*, she claimed, 'We have found the survival of Lughnasa at a hundred and ninety-five sites in Ireland ... Lughnasa was celebrated until recently on ninety-five heights and by ten lakes and five river banks.' Mountain tops, wells, river banks and lakes were all designated sacred areas for the primal rites.

The festival changed over the years – sacrificing

animals disappeared early in its evolution in Ireland – but many elements remained constant from generation to generation. The head of the family or the chief man of the community would always cut the first corn or wheat and offer it to Lugh. In return, Lugh gave the people his first fruit, the small dark blue bilberries growing wild on the hillside. The picking of bilberries has been the lasting custom of Lughnasa – they were looked on as a foretaste of the earth's fruitfulness and the god's bounty. Everyone ate them and some were always brought home to the old and infirm.

The Lughnasa Festival was so important in the lives of the people that Christianity had to adopt it or allow it to survive. MacNeill maintains:

> It could not crush it as it may have crushed observances at the other quarterly feasts ... It succeeded in turning the most important assemblies into Christian devotions ... but in taking them over it took over inevitably some of the old stories, altered only in making a saint, not a god, the people's champion. If ... it left a great number unconverted to Christian devotion, it succeeded in suppressing specifically pagan customs.

Dancing is, however, the most prominent and persistent element of the Lughnasa Festival in Ireland. Here is an oral account of the festival in 1942 from Gortahork in County Donegal:

> As I remember it, I heard the old people say that ... on the first Sunday of the month of Lughnasa ... was set out specially for the young people to go off to the hills as soon as the mid-day meal was eaten ... Then they would go here and there over the hill looking for

bilberries ... When they returned ... they had a strange custom. They all sat down on the hill-top and the boys began to make bracelets of bilberries for the girls. They had brought short threads in their pockets for the purpose ... Each man would compete with another as to which would make the best and prettiest bracelet for his own girl. When that was done, a man or maybe a girl would be named to sing a song. The melody would begin then and would go round from one to another, and anyone who had a note of music at all in his or her head would have to keep the fun going. After the singing they would begin dancing. According to the old talk, they had no instrument for music at all; they had to make do with lilting. In those days boys and girls were good at lilting and they would make enough music for those who were dancing ... When all was over then and they were preparing to go home, the girls would take off the bilberry bracelets and leave them on the hill-top. Whatever meaning was to that, none of the old people were able to tell me, but they all knew it and they heard from their elders that it was customary for them to do that. They would all come down then and go home. (from MacNeill, reprinted in the programme of the Abbey Theatre's première production)

The Stage-World

Locale
We are back in Ballybeg, but the Mundys' home is two miles outside the village, necessitating a long walk to reach any amenities. It isolates the family further in a county which, you will remember as a result of Partition,

is only joined to the rest of the Free State by a narrow
strip of land. Donegal's remoteness contributes to the
gravity of its economic condition, which is reflected
mainly in the dire financial situation of the Mundy family.
Their more affluent present or former neighbours have
either embraced modernisation (Austin Morgan) or
emigrated (Bernie O'Donnell and Brian McGuinness).
The period of the thirties is powerfully evoked through
references to popular culture, politics and historical
events; i.e., dance music and songs – always a potent
source of nostalgia – entertainers such as Fred Astaire,
Shirley Temple and Charlie Chaplin; political leaders
including De Valera, Mussolini and Gandhi; and the
Spanish Civil War.

Ballybeg is in the grip of the Lughnasa Festival. This is
manifest by two events which provide a background to
the daily life of the Mundys. First, the imminence of the
traditional harvest dance which, according to Miss Sophia
McLaughlin, is 'going to be just *supreme* this year' (p. 15).
The normally reticent Agnes is the one who suggests they
should all go, but when Kate sees Rose cavorting to
'Abyssinia' she panics and the whole wonderful idea is
quashed (p. 18). The other event has already occurred.
According to Rose,

> It was last Sunday week, the first night of the Festival
> of Lughnasa; and they were doing what they do every
> year up there in the black hills ... First they light a
> bonfire beside a spring well. Then they dance round it.
> Then they drive their cattle through the flames to
> banish the devil out of them ... And this year there
> was an extra big crowd of boys and girls. And they
> were off their heads with drink. And young Sweeney's

trousers caught fire and he went up like a torch. (pp. 22–3)

Kate has brought news that Sweeney is dying and has been anointed by the priest. Rose's story of residual pagan rites in the local area is, therefore, juxtaposed with the rites of Catholicism. We are immediately told by a very angry Kate that theirs is 'a Christian home, a Catholic home!' which has no room for such 'pagan practices' (p. 23). We learn later from Kate that young Sweeney's trousers did not catch fire, they 'were doing some devilish thing with a goat – some sort of sacrifice for the Lughnasa Festival; and Sweeney was so drunk he toppled into the middle of the bonfire' (p. 50). However, the Lughnasa fires continue to burn throughout the month of August. Rose tells us that some are still smouldering early in September and, although his legs will be scarred, the Sweeney boy is on the mend (p. 83).

As with the other Ballybeg plays, Friel creates a community which is introduced to us through report or reminiscence by the central characters. A whole cast of offstage characters are assembled here for you to imagine, as is the local countryside. The world of *Dancing at Lughnasa* also embraces London's cardboard city and more exotic, faraway places in Europe, Australia and Africa.

Setting

There is a composite set which Friel describes in some detail. Please look at these notes carefully. The furnishings in the room are austere, denoting the family's economic situation, but *'because this is the home of five women'* there are *'some gracious touches – flowers, pretty curtains, an attractive dresser arrangement, etc'*. I am going to quote from an article by Derek West in *Theatre Ireland* (spring 1990, p. 11) which describes the way the designer Joe Vanek created the setting for the original production. As this production was recreated in London and New York to huge popular and critical acclaim, the setting has become iconic and is now part of the theatrical folklore of the play. It demonstrates how a designer not only provides an environment in which the action of the play can take place but also interprets the play in visual terms, thus conveying meaning to an audience on several levels. West states that Vanek's design 'brings to the stage a striking image of the late summer that encompasses the major themes of the play'. He continues:

The set is dominated by a field of barley, climbing steeply above the kitchen and farmyard, where most of the action occurs. This superbly executed field ... is commanding, mesmerising – verging on the obtrusive – as if Vanek had an urge to translate a Monet painting onto the stage ... It is a constant visual presence, an attendant image of fertility, growth and, most poignantly, the promise of a fulfilment that is elusive and at best fitting for the main characters. Vanek's setting seems to draw its colouring from Africa ... rather than from Donegal ... This involves the audience in two juxtaposed worlds: that of tribal Uganda (with its own rhythms and ceremonies) and a rural Ireland clinging in folk memory to the vestiges of the pagan rites which are being stifled by the conventions of a thirties Catholic society. The pastel shades with which Vanek has painted the farmhouse, serve to underline the memory framework of the play ... The setting, albeit firmly naturalistic in much of its detail (the turf stack, the range, the iron, enamel jugs and buckets) is frequently bathed in a summer light, in a largely successful attempt to render atmosphere rather than fact.

Friel draws our attention to the clothes that the sisters wear, which '*reflect their lean circumstances*'. Note the specificity of particular items – drab, wrap-around overalls or aprons; wellingtons and large boots with untied laces. These are all character-based and will help you to build up a picture of each clearly defined sister. Father Jack receives particular attention. The '*magnificent and immaculate uniform of dazzling white*' that he wears in the opening tableau is one he wore briefly as a British Army chaplain. This is the Uncle Jack of the photograph and the '*resplendent*' figure of young Michael's memory (p. 2). The '*soiled and shabby*' version of the uniform appears towards the end of the play – 'Needs a bit of a clean up. Okawa's always dressing up in it' (p. 96). The deterioration in Jack's emblematic uniform reflects his fall from grace. Friel also describes Jack's appearance in his ordinary clothes (p. 24). They are much too big for him and quite unsuitable for the hot summer weather, but Jack is feeling the difference in climate and is suffering from malaria. In Act Two, although he looks fitter, his dress is even more '*bizarre*' (p. 63). Jack is completely at odds with his surroundings – forever the exile.

Another transformation involves Rose. For the most part she is dressed in a dowdy over-all and wellington boots, but when she goes to pick bilberries with Agnes she is wearing 'her good shoes ... blue cardigan and her good skirt' (p. 77). You will remember that Rose goes to meet Danny Bradley and when she returns to the house Friel states that the 'good' clothes *'have changed her appearance ... had we not seen the Rose of Act One, we might not now be immediately aware of her disability ... this might be any youngish country woman, carefully dressed, not unattractive, returning from a long walk on a summer day.'* It is what she does before she enters the house that breaks the illusion: *'... she puts her hand into one of the cans, takes a fistful of berries and thrusts the fistful into her mouth ... she wipes her mouth with her sleeve and the back of her hand ... she looks at her stained fingers ... wipes them on her skirt.'* Rose does all these movements *'calmly'* and *'naturally'* (pp. 79–80).

The surface naturalism of the play requires a number of household properties which are used throughout. These are familiar, everyday objects which we would normally take for granted. The sisters' impecunious situation, however, gives them a particular value and to some extent they are almost precious. Later we will look at how their use creates a kind of ritual out of the sisters' day-to-day existence, where these ordinary objects become ceremonial artefacts.

Marconi has a special place in the kitchen. Note how it got its name, and although the inventor's appellation is an apt one, 'Lugh' would be even more appropriate given the wireless's contribution to certain subversive activities which take place in the household. Despite Marconi's unreliability it provides an escape from the humdrum of the sisters' daily lives. From it emanates the seductive melodies of popular American dance music, the stirring notes of the ceilidh band and, an ironic touch, a three-second blast of 'The British Grenadiers'. Thus the wireless provides an organic source of music to accompany the different kinds of dancing presented in the play. Marconi is also a nod towards modernity and an important link with the outside world. Michael's kites carry a more obvious symbolic significance. They are present through-out the action but not fully revealed until the end. In the making they represent play and a kind of freedom, but the image they finally project is unsettling – a crude and grotesque intrusion into what should be an idyllic landscape.

It is interesting that in *Dancing at Lughnasa* Friel gives specific instructions about the light in terms of both focus and atmosphere. Here he is initiating the use of technology to tell the story rather than leaving it to his designer as he might have done in the past. It emphasises the fact that the visual elements of the play are of the utmost importance. In the stage-directions at the top of Act One he states that Michael '*is standing downstage in a pool of light*', thus isolating and highlighting him in the space. This image is reinforced by the blackness around him. The stage lighting is slowly brought in and up as he starts to speak – as he conjures the memory, the tableau emerges from the darkness. At the end of the monologue the lighting changes and the kitchen and garden '*are now lit as for a warm summer afternoon*'. Here the audience has been invited into the world of the play through the movement of the light. Friel is equally specific at the end of the play. As the final tableau forms and Michael begins his last monologue, '*the stage is lit in a very soft, golden light so that the tableau we see is almost, but not quite, in a haze*' (p. 99). The memory and the stage are bathed in a golden light but the effect is essentially hazy, elusive. The atmosphere is heightened by the 'dream music', and the sense of floating created by the gentle swaying of the group in the tableau. The audience should respond emotionally to these sensory elements. The combined effect is mesmeric and deeply moving.

The Characters

The five Mundy sisters are brilliantly delineated and beautifully drawn. Friel gives specific stage-directions about them (ages, dress, manner) but you should also look for internal evidence in the text. What do they say about each other, how to they perceive themselves, do the men provide any additional information? Each woman is given a precise and memorable individuality and yet together they form a cohesive group which embraces, protects and nurtures, and also reflects both the loyalties and tensions of sisterhood. All have their own distinctive voice but collectively, through expression and accent, they have a Donegal sound. This distinguishes them from Jack, who has virtually lost his Irish accent, and Gerry, who has standard English pronunciation. Unlike the men they have never ventured outside the narrow confines of their locality. The sisters have been brought up in a good Catholic home by strict parents – Maggie refers to 'Daddy' and his probable disapproval of her bike ride to the dance (p. 28) and Kate to a 'saintly' Mother 'who knew she was going straight to heaven' (p. 54). The sisters have dignity and courage but their sense of fun, appetite for life and sexuality have been muted by their circumstances. They no longer have any expectations.

Kate is the eldest and the breadwinner – she has been a schoolteacher for many years. Her strait-laced attitudes and prim manner belie a wry sense of humour. She is, however, tormented by the prospect of scandal which might cost her her job and thus lose the family's livelihood. She thoroughly disapproves of Gerry yet she tolerates him for Chris's sake – 'Of course ask him in. And give the creature his tea' (p. 36). She was involved locally in the Irish war of independence against the British and it is interesting to speculate in what way. Whatever passion she had for nationalist politics at that time, her energies now go into her work, providing for her family as matriarch and upholding the Catholic faith. However, there is a link between her faith and her politics; she says to Gerry: 'It's a sorry day for Ireland when we send young men off to Spain to fight for godless Communism' (p. 73). 'Agnes was too notionate to work in a factory' (p. 83) and Jack engaged in 'his own distinctive spiritual search' (p. 84) are phrases which Kate coins to excuse or justify the human frailty of those near to her. She is fiercely protective of her loved ones, a sensitive woman who has suppressed her emotions through a sense of propriety and duty. But to Maggie she reveals her fears about the future, and Rose in particular (pp. 50–51); and we get a glimpse of what might happen if she let go (p. 69). Michael says she was 'inconsolable' for months after brother Jack died.

Maggie is in her late thirties and looks after the house. Note her heavy boots which she is obliged to wear unlaced. She has a weakness for men and Wild Woodbines but only the latter is available. Maggie is a spirited woman with a tremendous sense of fun, which is, of course, also a means of survival, her bubbling vitality holding off despair. Her earthy wit and jokey songs punctuate the action throughout the play. Maggie is a romantic at heart and she is the first to 'rebel', uninhibitedly leading their pagan dance. She lacks the grace and beauty of her younger sisters, Agnes and Chris, but her cheerful pragmatism and generosity of spirit make her an extremely attractive character. Her ebullient manner does not, however, hide her pain at lost opportunities and the prospect of a bleak future. Note her vulnerability as she watches Chris and Gerry dance (pp. 46–7). She is compassionate and it is to Maggie that Kate, the supposed strong one, turns to for support (above); and in the panic that ensues at the news of Rose's 'disappearance', it is Maggie who takes charge (pp. 78–9).

Agnes comes next, in her mid-thirties. She and Rose earn a little money by knitting from home and Maggie says she is clever with her hands. Friel is specific about Agnes's role as Rose's 'special protector'. Agnes is shy and introspective, often hiding secret longings behind an enigmatic smile. Note that she reads romantic novels and is a gifted dancer; Friel says that she moves the most sensuously of all the sisters. She is obviously in love with Gerry and comes alive in his arms as they dance. Of all the sisters she, as the most introspective, seems the least likely to leave home. However, Agnes has an inner strength and when faced with the prospect of the knitting factory, where she knows her sister will never be employed, she leaves the family home taking Rose with her. The farewell note is written in Agnes's '*resolute hand*'. As she said of the dance, 'I'm game' (p. 16).

Rose is 'simple'. Her disability is akin to that of Manus and Sarah in *Translations*, denoting that all is not well in the society. But Rose has an extraordinary directness and determination, coupled with a childlike innocence, which gives her a special quality. This is offset by her unpredictability, indiscretion, gaucheness and sometimes boisterous behaviour. She is convinced that she is loved by Danny Bradley – 'He calls me his Rosebud . . . I love him, Aggie.' There is a dark aspect to this supposed relationship, however, which is reflected in the sisters' response when Rose reveals that she might be meeting him (p. 7). Her sudden disappearance from the bilberry-picking expedition causes real panic amongst the sisters (pp. 76–8). Rose is extremely vulnerable and needs constant protection and, despite Agnes's obvious valiant efforts to save her, we can imagine her sinking into a life of destitution (pp. 83–4).

Chris, at twenty-six, is the youngest and the only sister to have borne a child. There is only one brief mention of the shame brought on the family by Chris's youthful indiscretion – she was nineteen. She is life-loving, with a trusting nature which has been severely tested by the easy charm and empty promises of Gerry Evans. It is hinted that his careless rejection of her caused her great anguish, 'sobbing', 'lamenting in the middle of the night' and a 'collapse into one of her depressions' (p. 50). However, she appears to bear no grudge towards him and, for the brief time they are together, indulges his fantasies and her own day-dreams. Her 'marriage' to Gerry is a source of joy and makes the grief at his leaving bearable – the acceptance of loss that comes with maturity. She is a good mother to Michael. Jack refers to him as a love-child, which is exactly what he is.

Father Jack is a wreck. Once hugely admired and respected by his sisters, he is now the second child in the family needing constant care. He is even learning the language again. He is also in disgrace, having 'gone native' in Uganda and thus been rejected by the Church and the political establishment. His presence in Ballybeg is a threat to the sisters, particularly Kate, who loses her job at the school because of his irrevocable lapse. In a sense he is a shocking figure – a Catholic missionary from a loving family who has been 'translated' into something deeply African. He is now the 'Irish Outcast' (p. 55). The customs and rituals he lives by are unrecognisable to his sisters, as is the man. It is important to remember, nevertheless, that Jack has worked in a leper colony in a remote village in Uganda for twenty-five years. We cannot dismiss this commitment. Also his conversion to the African way of life is informed by a deep love for the people, as represented by Okawa.

Jack has, however, carried with him all the time an image of his mother and sisters that he compares to a photograph in his mind. In his reminiscence of the last time he saw Chris, he remembers 'Mother lifting you up as the train was pulling out of the station and catching your hand and waving it at me' (p. 54). He recalls the other sisters, too, but what lingers in his memory is the expression, or lack of it, on his mother's face, for she 'showed nothing'. The manner of her farewell has affected him deeply. This fleeting insight into the family's past is both disturbing and moving.

Gerry Evans is a 'Tinker! . . . Loafer! Wastrel', according to Kate. This ne'er-do-well has another family in South Wales, comprising a wife and three children. He is the archetypal travelling salesman leading a double life, one at home and another on the road. He is, however, undeniably attractive and tells great tall-stories which make Chris laugh. In fact his rakish charm affects all the sisters – note their various responses on his arrival (p. 34). He is also an expert dancer, a gift which brings with it an air of romance, a factor otherwise sadly lacking in the life of the Mundy sisters. His enlistment in the International Brigade is motivated more by his spirit of adventure and the conspicuous failure of his career than by his belief in a political ideology, and the circumstance of his 'invaliding out' is entirely in character (p. 85). His injury put an end to his dancing but he did savour the role of 'maimed veteran' for the rest of his various lives.

Dramatic Structure

The play has a simple two-act structure which focuses on two afternoons, separated by three weeks, in August and September respectively. This accommodates the 'present' action of the play. However, the notion of memory is explored through the role of Michael and his central memory of those two afternoons and, more peripherally although still organic to the Mundys' story, the recollections of Maggie and Jack: her experience at the Ardstraw dance, and his farewell to his mother and sisters twenty-five years ago. We are also projected forwards in time by Michael's narration to learn more of the family's history.

THE NARRATOR Friel has already used the structural device of the split character in *Philadelphia, Here I Come!* and his use of monologue in other works is prolific and effective. Here he combines both elements to create a narrator figure that stands outside the action and also participates in it as a defined character, albeit represented as a voice only. Again it is a device which works beautifully in the theatre but is less satisfying on the page. As the narrator, Michael is a storyteller drawing the audience in and yet distancing them from the memory. Michael is also remembering at a distance and he knows that his memory owes more to atmosphere than fact. The narrative tone is important here: it should not be omniscient; a light touch and objectivity are essential. The pace of the narration is also a consideration; the man Michael belongs to a different world to that of his aunts, uncle and father, and his monologues should not be obtrusive. The role requires the utmost sensitivity and tact in the playing.

The representation of the child is more structurally complex. He is in the scene and yet absent from it. The sisters talk to him as though he were physically there, allowing space onstage for his presence. They engage in dialogue with the boy, but it is Michael the narrator who responds and in his normal voice as a man. Friel sets up the convention first with Maggie, and his precise stage-directions show how it is to be implemented: '*No dialogue with the Boy Michael must ever be addressed directly to adult Michael, the narrator. Here, for example, Maggie has her back to the narrator ...*' (p. 9). Michael as narrator is therefore able to observe the scene in which he is participating as the boy, thus creating a double distancing. It encourages the audience's involvement in the story but denies them empathy. It is *Michael's* memory. We experience it as observers through him. We are, however, susceptible to the atmosphere, which is simultaneously embracing and elusive.

Act One

We know nothing about Michael the man; his occupation, whether he is married or single, etc., even his age is indeterminate, although Friel defines him as 'young'. This does not really matter. It is his memory that is all-important and something which is beyond time, eternal. He is not a constant presence onstage – he disappears occasionally, reappearing as the child or to resume his role as narrator. The first monologue establishes the convention and, visually juxtaposed with the tableau, introduces time, place, characters and events. The two major events for Michael are the arrival of Marconi and its magical effect on his mother and aunts, and Uncle Jack's homecoming, which turns out to be very different from what he imagined. Michael also expresses his sense of unease: 'And even though I was only a child of seven at the time I know I had ... some awareness of a widening breach between what seemed to be and what was, of things changing too quickly before my eyes, of becoming what they ought not to be' (p. 2). It is not until the end of the monologue that he mentions the two visits by his father, Gerry Evans, who he was able to 'observe' for the first time in his life.

We have already looked at the way Friel introduces the character of the boy, but it is important to note when the scenes take place and what they are about. The scene with Maggie establishes the emblems of the kites, Maggie's running gag of the riddles and the easy joshing relationship between aunt and nephew. The second 'boy' scene with Kate is preceded by Michael's second monologue, in which he gives information about Kate's political activity and further details of Uncle Jack. The photograph is an important metaphor – the semblance of the 'radiant' and 'splendid' Uncle Jack as he once was is compared to the 'reality' that we see onstage, both of which are filtered through Michael's memory. Michael also tells us of the esteem in which brother Jack was held by the family, the parish and the county; how his sisters prayed and saved for his mission, the 'sacrifices they made willingly, joyously' so that money was sent to him at Christmas and for his birthday; and of the stories that would appear about 'our own leper priest' in the *Donegal Enquirer*. Uncle Jack's fame raised the status of the family in the eyes of the parish, which 'must have helped my aunts to bear the shame Mother brought on the household by having me – as it was called then – out of wedlock' (p. 11).

Michael speaks this last sentence just before Kate enters. It would have been 'proper' Kate – the family's figure of moral rectitude – who would have felt the greatest shame. However, we see that now her relationship with the boy is one of delight in him and pride in his achievement. Friel says, '*her face lights up with pleasure. She watches him for a few seconds. Then she goes to him ... She catches his head between her hands and kisses the crown of his head.*' Kate takes a great interest in the kites, gives him the present of the spinning-top, which she can probably ill-afford, and promises to read to him from the new library book with the coloured pictures. Before she leaves, she kisses the top of his head again and says: 'Call me the moment you're ready to fly them. I wouldn't miss that for all the world' – and you believe her. She goes straight into the house to tell Christina and the others that Michael is making two kites. The boy is surrounded by love (p. 12).

Michael exits when the conversation moves on to other topics. He re-emerges to play the third boy-scene with Maggie (pp. 19–20). This scene is all about imagination and pretence – the fox having a conversation with Maggie and asking after Michael; the imaginary creature in her hand and its 'flight' as she frees it; the wonderful colours of the imaginary bird which Maggie finally lets on was all 'in his mind'.

Michael is then absent from the stage for some time, but the boy is kept in the audience's mind's eye by references to him in the dialogue: he disappears from the garden (p. 32); Gerry spies him at the bottom of the lane, and he can also see Michael watching him and his mother from behind a bush (p. 29). The narrator Michael enters when Kate is in tears and confides in Maggie that she worries about Rose most of all: 'If I died – if I lost my job – if this house were broken up – what would become of Rosie?' (pp. 50–51). He becomes boy Michael '*at his kites*' for the scene with his mother. To begin with the boy will not talk about his father, but his mother's enthusiasm eventually elicits questions as to when he will return. The scene really belongs to Chris, though, to show how excited she is about Gerry's visit and how much she wants to share her joy with her son.

In his third monologue, at the end of Act One, Michael picks up on Kate's forebodings (p. 58). He hints at another reason for Uncle Jack's return, which will cost Kate her job at the school. Michael also speaks of Agnes and Rose's departure, something that Kate 'couldn't have foreseen'. This news is deeply unsettling because it is so unexpected. It strikes a dissonant chord which is accentuated when Jack picks up two pieces of wood from the boy's kite and starts to beat out a rhythm that '*gives him pleasure*'. Jack's shuffle to the rhythm becomes a dance which is strangely at odds with the harmony implicit in Michael's description of his mother's 'marriage'. While the other sisters watch Jack, Chris '*has her eyes closed, her face raised, her mouth slightly open; remembering*' the 'ceremony' which Michael describes in lyrical detail (p. 59). However, the scene ends with Kate taking the sticks from Jack and leading him off for his walk. Michael's monologue foreshadows the changes that will take place, moving the action forward into the second half of the play.

Act Two

The boy Michael has only one scene here. When the second half opens, Michael is downstage-left watching and listening to Maggie as she works and sings. The scene with the boy, however, takes place in the kitchen, where the imagined child sits at the table. He is far more talkative and forthcoming and Maggie's jokey manner changes when he talks of the bike his daddy has bought him. She knows all about Gerry Evans's promises. Might he keep this one or will the child be hurt? Or does it denote a development in Gerry's relationship with Chris? We learn later that Gerry 'visited us occasionally, perhaps once a year. Each time he was on the brink of a new career. And each time he proposed to Mother and promised me a new bike' (p. 85).

In his penultimate narration Michael draws all the strands of the story together and takes us forward in time (pp. 83–6). The hardship and suffering that Agnes and Rose will experience is almost impossible to comprehend in the golden glow of the Lughnasa summer, but we know the stark brutality of their ending to be true. Uncle Jack will die within the year, although he appears to be making a full recovery, leaving Kate inconsolable in her grief. And Gerry Evans, the eternal romantic, turns out to be a complete fraud. The audience experiences the final scenes of the play in the light of this knowledge, which shows the Mundys' fleeting moments of joy to be even more fragile. Michael's final speech also expresses this fragility. He tells us the fate of those who were left – his mother, Maggie and Kate – and admits: 'and when my time came to go away, in the selfish way of young men I was happy to escape' (p. 99). The tableau forms, the music comes in and here Michael tries to capture his memory of that afternooon, bewitched and haunted by the mirage of sound which comes from the dream music that is both 'heard and imagined'. The picture of the family group also reaches us in a kind of haze. They sway gently to the rhythmic music and we are left with an image which takes us beyond words, to the dance at 'the very heart of life'.

Dancing, Ritual and Ceremony

Dancing is the central metaphor of the play, but as it is structurally and thematically linked in the text to ritual and ceremony I think it helpful to look at all these elements together.

Marconi's Voodoo

Michael introduces this idea in his first narration: how he witnessed the wireless's magic 'derange those kind, sensible women and transform them into shrieking strangers' (p. 2). The notion of dance as a release and escape is introduced when Agnes suggests that they should all go to the local harvest hop. She has £5 saved and generously offers to pay for them all: 'How many years has it been since we were at the harvest dance? – at any dance? And I don't care how young they are, how drunk and dirty and sweaty they are. I want to dance, Kate. It's the Festival of Lughnasa. I'm only thirty-five. I want to dance' (pp. 17–18). Look at the excitement generated in the dialogue, the pace and shifting focus, as the women discuss what they should wear (pp. 17–18). But Kate's propriety overrules the consensus and the sisters are reduced to silence.

We then have a dance remembered, triggered by Kate's news of her meeting with Bernie O'Donnell. Note Friel's stage-direction, which shows the effect of this upon

Maggie, who '*goes to the window and looks out so that the others cannot see her face. She holds her hands, covered with flour, out from her body*' (p. 26). If you look at the description of the set you will see that the position of this window is 'out front', so Maggie is looking directly at the audience. She stands there to tell her memory of the dance. This is wonderfully evocative and poignant as we recognise the injustice not only of the judges' rigged verdict but also that of Maggie's life. She remains motionless, '*staring out of the window, seeing nothing*', as Chris replaces the battery in Marconi and switches the wireless on. There follows a sequence of joy and terror, at once a celebration and a scream of rage, as all the sisters abandon themselves to the wild Irish music.

The shock of recognition and the startling effect that this dance has in the theatre is impossible to describe – it has to be experienced. However, you must try to imagine the impact that is created by the sound of the loud, raucous music, the yelps of the women combined with the thudding of their feet on the wooden floor, and the stage-picture of the normally demure sisters charged with a demonic energy. Friel builds the dance, starting from Maggie's defiant gesture with the flour, followed by Chris's tossing on of Jack's surplus, until all the sisters are involved. Each has their own particular form of expression, with Kate most recognisably drawing on traditional Irish steps. Apart from her initial yell, Kate makes no sound, dancing '*alone, totally concentrated, totally private*', whereas the other sisters keep up a continuous chorus of shouts, calls and snatches of song to accompany their dance. Friel indicates that Kate's dance weaves '*a pattern of action that is out of character and at the same time ominous of some deep and true emotion*'. Moreover,

'*With this too loud music, this pounding beat, this shouting – calling – singing, this parodic reel, there is a sense of order being consciously subverted, of the women consciously and crudely caricaturing themselves, indeed of near-hysteria being induced*' (p. 30).

It is important that this climactic moment occurs early in the first half of the play because our subsequent view of the sisters, individually and as a group, will be informed by this display. It reveals their deep-seated desire for release from repression of all kinds. It is akin to the pagan rites of Lughnasa which Kate has earlier dismissed with horror as 'no concern of ours' (p. 23). Yet here is Maggie, '*a white-faced, frantic dervish*', and Chris, a sacrilegious figure, dancing recklessly in a priest's vestment. The stage has been filled with the creative energy of these marvellous women, whose personal development has been stunted by their circumstances. The dance has released the life-force and provided a form of expression for their deepest passions which convention has continually denied them.

Strictly Ballroom

'Strictly ballroom', says Gerry when Chris asks him what kind of dancing he teaches. As the music drifts from the radio – the lush melody of 'Dancing in the Dark' – he suddenly takes her in his arms and dances. They are good together – '*He suddenly swings her round and dances her lightly, elegantly across the garden*' (p. 46). While this goes on, Maggie watches from the window, Agnes concentrates on her knitting and Kate pretends to read the newspaper. These responses say a great deal about the sisters and their reaction to Chris in the arms of her man. Unable to deny her curiosity any longer, Kate '*flings the*

paper aside and joins Maggie at the window' (p. 46). As
Kate watches them her attitude changes completely:
'That's the only thing that Evans creature could ever do
well – was dance. (*Pause.*) And look at her, the fool. For
God's sake, would you look at that fool of a woman?
(*Pause.*) Her whole face alters when she's happy, doesn't
it? (*Pause.*) They dance so well together. They're such a
beautiful couple. (*Pause.*) She's as beautiful as Bernie
O'Donnell any day, isn't she?' (p. 47). It is in the active
pauses that Kate's responses shift. The pauses are also a
vital part of the rhythm of the speech, which is working
with the rhythm of the music – a beautiful melody and
evocative sound – and the dance.

Look at the structure of the whole scene. It switches
between the couple's dialogue and that of the watchers
but the focus is always on the dancers, with the music a
constant factor in the background. Agnes says very little
but her distress is evident from her outburst to Kate after
the couple have danced off: 'Do you ever listen to
yourself, Kate? You are such a damned righteous bitch!
And his name is Gerry! – Gerry! – Gerry!' And on the
point of tears she runs away (p. 49). Michael tells us of an
even more magical dance in his narration at the end of the
act. While his mother sits with her eyes closed and mouth
slightly open, remembering, Michael tells of her 'marriage' to Gerry, witnessed by the unseen sisters: 'And this
time it was a dance without music; just there in ritual
circles round and round that square and then down the
lane and back up again; slowly, formally, with easy
deliberation.' Look at Michael's description of their body
language and how totally absorbed they are in each other.
This time there was 'no singing, no melody, no words.
Only the swish and whisper of their feet across the grass.'

The memory here is so distilled and expressed with such ravishing simplicity that the image, although not seen, is vividly remembered (p. 59). But juxtaposed with these tender memories is a disturbing element. In the background, Uncle Jack is dancing in time to his tattoo, a different rhythm, ritual and ceremony. Perfect harmony in Ballybeg is no longer possible. Kate's forebodings and Michael's unease are manifest in more than cracked mirrors, single magpies and, later, the dead rooster.

The last ballroom dance – the sophisticated 'Anything Goes' – occurs after we are told by Michael of Agnes and Rose's fate on the streets of London. So, despite the upbeat tempo of the music the sequence is tinged with grief. Gerry has always had a soft spot for Agnes – note how he asks after her on his first visit – and here he takes the opportunity to dance with her. Friel indicates that the sound should be brought up, filling the theatre, almost turning the sequence into a production number (p. 90). They dance together *With style and with easy elegance*. This is Agnes's forte – remember Friel's note about her grace and sensuality in the Irish reel – and Cole Porter's witty lyrics sung by Gerry *directly to her face* have a sexual charge which goes beyond the romantic. Chris instinctively senses their physical rapport – remember she sees them move but does not hear them speak or sing from her position at the window – and, after Maggie decides to join the party, she curtails any further developments by turning the radio off (p. 92).

Work Rituals

Both the Irish reel and the ballroom dancing are set against the ritual of the sisters' daily work. There are many stage-directions which indicate these menial tasks. Please do not skim over them but look to see precisely what tasks each character carries out during the course of the play – fires are stoked, bread is made, clothes are ironed, and so on. The knitting is also important here. The sisters handle the utensils, tools and ingredients with respect – when you have very little you value what you have – and show considerable expertise and skill in the implementation of their several tasks. Each of these has their own form, shape and rhythm, and when put together create a pattern which reflects the texture of the sisters' lives. The duties and work may seem boring and mundane but the sisters invest them all with care and consideration and, cumulatively, they acquire a dignity that is very moving.

Rynagan Ceremonies

We have already looked at the nature of the rites taking place in the black hills above Ballybeg, the remnants of pagan practices associated with the ancient Festival of Lughnasa of which the harvest dance and the picking of bilberries are the more innocuous customs. These pagan practices preceded Christianity, the rites of which now take precedent in the community in the form of the rituals and ceremonies of the Catholic Church. The vestiges of the Lughnasa rituals and the Mundy sisters' wild dance suggest, however, that dark subversive forces still lie beneath the strictures and decorum of good Catholic households and religious orthodoxy.

Jack has been living in a community – the beliefs and culture of which he has adopted – where there is no division between the religious and the secular. Jack is reminded of the rituals in Ryanga by Maggie commenting that she is going to wring the rooster's neck one day: 'That's what we do ... when we want to please the spirits – or appease them: we kill a rooster or a young goat' (p. 55). He has, however, forgotten the name of the word for the event. Friel thus draws our attention to the word 'ceremony' when Jack triumphantly remembers it (p. 56). Gradually we learn more about his way of life in the African village and leper colony – love-children, men with several wives, the medicine man, and so on – until finally he describes two of the most important ceremonies.

Okawa – Jack's house-boy, friend, mentor, councillor – is instrumental in gathering the community (p. 65). Up to four hundred people meet in the common in the centre of the village. Two ceremonies take place at harvest time – the Festival of the New Yam and the Festival of the Sweet Casava. These involve ritual sacrifice; the cutting and anointing of the yams and casava which are passed round in communal bowls;

> Then the incantation – a chant, really – that expresses our gratitude and that also acts as a rhythm or percussion for the ritual dance. And then, when the thanksgiving is over, the dance continues. And the interesting thing is that it grows naturally into a secular celebration; so almost imperceptibly the religious ceremony ends and the community celebration takes over. And that part of the ceremony is a real spectacle. We light fires round the periphery of the circle; and we paint our faces with coloured powders; and we sing local songs; and we drink palm wine. And then we dance – and dance – and dance – children, men, women, most of them lepers, many of them with misshapen limbs, with missing limbs – dancing, believe it or not, for days on end! It is the most wonderful sight you have ever seen! (pp. 66–7).

This vision fills Kate with alarm, but Maggie deflects any discomfort she herself might feel by making a joke about lepers trying to do the military two-step. Jack has 'gone native' and will never say Mass again, but the picture he paints is nothing to do with the crude, cruel and garishly painted images on Michael's kites but one of wholeness, of a community at peace with itself. Jack has embraced 'the other' and been accepted by them. The supposed converter, the missionary of white civilisation, has become converted to an old world of ceremony and ancient wisdom. He is an irritant to the colonisers and has been got rid of. The colonial ceremony that Jack plays out with Gerry, takes us into the final dance of the play. It involves the exchange of hats, and for it Jack puts on his once-resplendent uniform. He demonstrates the business with the hats – 'a symbolic distancing of yourself from what you once possessed' and a 'formal rejection of what you once had' – and Jack now wears Gerry's straw hat while Gerry dons the white tricorn (pp. 96–7). The kites are revealed and the characters move into their final positions.

This tableau echoes rather than replicates the first one. Things have changed: most notably the condition of Jack's ceremonial dress and Gerry's tricorn; Rose and Agnes have swapped positions; Kate is now quietly crying; and there is the addition of the cruel, grinning faces on the kites. We are accustomed to the state of the battered uniform but the kites' faces are a new feature – a disturbing element in the golden garden. But very softly, '*just audible*', the music – '*It is Time to Say Goodnight*' – is faded in. Not from Marconi this time, but a sweet sound that will drift through the theatre. The group '*sways very slightly from side to side ... the movement is so minimal that we cannot be quite certain if it is happening or if we imagine it'* (pp. 99–100). The image shimmers and floats.

Wordless Ceremony

We have touched on this image of memory several times already but I should like you to consider it now as the moment where Friel takes us beyond language, 'to whisper private and sacred things, to be in touch with otherness'. Michael is searching for that mystical wholeness which Jack finds in the Ryangan dances and Chris and Gerry experience briefly in the silent dance of their 'marriage'. Is it there on that afternoon in Ballybeg with his family bathed in the golden hazy light? He remembers it as dancing 'with eyes half closed because to open them would break the spell'. Does he find 'the very heart of life and all its hopes ... in those assuaging notes and those hushed rhythms and in those silent and hypnotic movements'? Words are no longer necessary – we are left with the haunting music and the dance, a mysterious and magical moment.

Endnote

In *Philadelphia, Here I Come!* Gareth O'Donnell seeks to take into exile 'Just the memory of it ... just the memory ... distilled of all its coarseness; and what's left is going to be precious, precious gold.' In *Dancing at Lughnasa*, Michael, another exile, seems to have achieved this. Like Gareth, who tries to capture Madge in his imaginary film, Michael also has a visual image, reminiscent of a family photograph, which he retains in his mind's eye. But unlike *Philadelphia, Here I Come!* where silence is 'the enemy', here in *Dancing at Lughnasa* it is a state of grace. In the final moments of this extraordinary play we are transported to the very heart of the dance of life.

Textual Notes

4 Benito Mussolini – (1883–1945) Fascist dictator of Italy, 1922–43. From 1935 an aggressive foreign policy in Abyssinia and Spain was at first successful and in June 1940 he entered the war on the side of Hitler. Rose and Maggie are singing about very topical events in their songs.

5 Mahatma Gandhi – (1869–1948) Indian patriot, social reformer and moral teacher. In the movement for Indian independence after 1914 he dominated Congress, instituted civil disobedience, and advocated non-violence. Another example of opposition to British colonial rule.

6 whin-bush – furze/gorse bush.

– quinine – a medicine used in treating malaria.

– scut – a contemptible man.

8 'The Isle of Capri' – a popular song made famous by Al Bowley.

20 Indian meal – grain ground to a coarse powder.

28 workhouse – a public institution for paupers.

44 Spanish Civil War – started on 18 July 1936 and is, therefore, a very recent event.

45 'Dancing in the Dark' – a romantic popular song, now a classic of its kind.

55 Kampala – capital of Uganda.

67 Gilbert and Sullivan – W. S. Gilbert (1836–1911) and Arthur Sullivan (1842–1900) – librettist and composer, respectively, of popular light operas.

75 gansey – jumper.

85 Fred Astaire – famous exponent of the kind of dance performed in the play.

88 'Anything Goes' – title song of a musical show, now a standard classic.

91 Shirley Temple – singing and dancing child-star of Hollywood films.

95 jouking – sneaking.

97 Charlie Chaplin – (1880–1977) first international screen-star, best known for his character of the little tramp. Gerry is imitating his famous walk.

99 'It's Time to Say Goodnight' – it is impossible to describe just how perfect this is for the final sequence. It is, however, a rare piece and difficult to come by.

Chronology

1950 Brian Friel begins writing short stories.
1958 First radio plays produced by BBC Belfast.
1959 Regular contributor to *The New Yorker*.
     The Doubtful Paradise, first stage-play, at the
     Ulster Group Theatre, Belfast.
1962 *The Enemy Within*, Abbey Theatre (then at the
     Queen's), Dublin.
     First collection of short stories, *The Saucer of
     Larks*.
1963 Spends six months with Tyrone Guthrie at the new
     Guthrie Theater, Minneapolis.
1964 *Philadelphia, Here I Come!*, Gaiety Theatre,
     Dublin; Helen Hayes Theater, New York, 1965;
     Lyric Theatre, London, 1967.
1966 Second collection of short stories, *The Gold in the
     Sea*.
     The Loves of Cass Maguire, Helen Hayes Theater,
     New York; Abbey Theatre, Dublin, 1967.
1967 *Lovers*, Gate Theatre, Dublin; Lincoln Center,
     New York, 1968; Fortune Theatre, London, 1968.
1968 *Crystal and Fox*, Gaiety Theatre, Dublin; Mark
     Taper Forum, Los Angeles.
1969 *The Mundy Scheme*, Olympia Theatre, Dublin;
     Royale Theater, New York.
1971 *The Gentle Island*, Olympia Theatre, Dublin;
     Peacock Theatre, Dublin, 1989.
1973 *The Freedom of the City*, Royal Court Theatre,

London; Abbey Theatre, Dublin; Alvin Theater,
New York, 1974.

1975 *Volunteers*, Abbey Theatre, Dublin.

1977 *Living Quarters*, Abbey Theatre, Dublin.

1979 *Aristocrats*, Abbey Theatre, Dublin; Hampstead
Theatre, London, 1988; Manhattan Theater Club,
New York, 1989; Gate Theatre, Dublin, 1990.
Faith Healer, Longacre Theater, New York; Abbey
Theatre, Dublin, 1980; Royal Court Theatre,
London, 1981.

1980 Co-founder with Stephen Rea of Field Day Theatre
Company. *Translations* opens in Derry;
Hampstead Theatre and the National Theatre,
London, 1981; Manhattan Theater Club, New
York, 1981.

1981 His translation of Chekhov's *Three Sisters* opens
in Derry; Royal Court Theatre, London.
Ewart-Biggs Prize.
American-Irish Foundation Literary Award.

1982 *The Communication Cord* opens in Derry;
Hampstead Theatre, London, 1983.

1983 Doctor of Letters, National University of Ireland.

1986 Editor of *The Last of the Name*.

1987 Adaptation of Turgenev's novel *Fathers and
Sons*, Royal National Theatre, London; Long
Wharf Theater, USA; Gate Theatre, Dublin,
1988.

1988 *Making History* opens in Derry; Royal National
Theatre, London; Gaiety Theatre, Dublin.
Doctor of Letters, University of Ulster.

1989 BBC Radio devotes a six-play season to Friel.
Sunday Independent/Irish Life Arts Award for
Theatre.

1990 *Dancing at Lughnasa*, Abbey Theatre, Dublin;
Royal National Theatre, London.

1991 *Dancing at Lughnasa*, Phoenix Theatre, London,
and Plymouth Theater, New York, wins Tony
Awards for Best Play, Best Director and Best
Supporting Actress.
The London Vertigo, Gate Theatre at Andrew's
Lane, Dublin.

1992 *A Month in the Country*, Gate Theatre, Dublin.

1993 *Wonderful Tennessee*, Abbey Theatre, Dublin;
Plymouth Theater, New York.
Dancing at Lughnasa, Abbey Theatre national
tour, Australian tour.

1994 *Molly Sweeney*, Gate Theatre, Dublin; Almeida
Theatre, London.

1997 *Give Me Your Answer, Do!*, Abbey Theatre,
Dublin.

1998 *Give Me Your Answer, Do!*, Hampstead Theatre,
London.
Friel's version of Chekhov's *Uncle Vanya*, Gate
Theatre, Dublin.
Film of *Dancing at Lughnasa*, screenplay by Frank
McGuinness, is released.

1999 Friel Festival: including *The Freedom of the City*
and *Dancing at Lughnasa* at the Abbey Theatre,
Living Quarters and *Making History* at the
Peacock Theatre (all National Theatre
productions), *Aristocrats* at the Gate Theatre, the
Royal Shakespeare Company's production of *A
Month in the Country* at the Gaiety Theatre and
Lovers, Winners and Losers at Andrew's Lane
Theatre, all in Dublin; and *Give Me Your Answer,
Do!* at the Lyric Theatre, Belfast. Other events

included *Brian Friel – A Celebration* at the
National Library, Dublin, an exhibition of letters,
playscripts, photographs and posters presented by
the National Theatre Literary Department and
Archive in association with the National Library of
Ireland.

Friel received a Lifetime Achievement Arts Award on the
occasion of his seventieth birthday.

Select Bibliography

Works by Brian Friel

The Saucer of Larks. New York: Doubleday, 1962

Philadelphia, Here I Come!. London: Faber and Faber, 1965

The Gold in the Sea. New York: Doubleday, 1966

The Loves of Cass Maguire. New York: Noonday Press, 1966

Lovers. London: Faber and Faber, 1969

The Saucer of Larks: Stories of Ireland. London: Arrow Books, 1969

Crystal and Fox. London: Faber and Faber, 1970

Crystal and Fox and *The Mundy Scheme*. New York: Farrar, Strauss and Giroux, 1970

The Gentle Island. London: Davis-Poynter, 1973

The Freedom of the City. London: Faber and Faber, 1974

The Enemy Within. Newark, Del.: Proscenium Press, 1975

Living Quarters. London: Faber and Faber, 1978

Volunteers. London: Faber and Faber, 1978

Selected Stories. Dublin: Gallery Press, 1980

Aristocrats. Dublin: Gallery Press, 1980

Faith Healer. London: Faber and Faber, 1980

Translations. London: Faber and Faber, 1980

Three Sisters (Chekhov). Dublin: Gallery Press, 1981

American Welcome. In Stanley Richards, ed., *Best Short Plays 1981*. Radnor, Pa.: Chilton Book Co., 1981

The Diviner. Dublin: O'Brien Press, 1983

The Communication Cord. London: Faber and Faber, 1983

Selected Plays. London: Faber and Faber, 1984

Fathers and Sons. London: Faber and Faber, 1987

Making History. London: Faber and Faber, 1988

Dancing at Lughnasa. London: Faber and Faber, 1990

The London Vertigo. Oldcastle: Gallery Press, 1990

A Month in the Country. Oldcastle: Gallery Press, 1992

Wonderful Tennessee. Oldcastle: Gallery Press, 1993

Molly Sweeney. Oldcastle: Gallery Press, 1994

Brian Friel: Essays, Diaries, Interviews: 1964–1999, ed. Christopher Murray, London: Faber and Faber, 1999. A timely and extremely useful collection, with an excellent introduction by Murray, which gives many fascinating insights into Friel's life and work. Also a celebration of 'one of the best playwrights in the world' (*Irish Times*). Several of the interviews, extracts from diaries and programme notes have been referred to in this Guide where the original sources are acknowledged. Essential reading as a companion to the plays.

Secondary Sources

Dantanus, Ulf, *Brian Friel, A Study*, London: Faber and Faber, 1988. A concise, informative guide to Friel's work to 1988, with relevant biographical details, surveys of his early short stories and radio plays, and criticism of his successful stage-plays, with a general introduction that places Friel in the context of the modern Irish literary tradition.

Deane, Seamus, Introduction, *Selected Plays of Brian Friel*, London: Faber and Faber, 1984. A notable introduction to *Philadelphia, Here I Come!*, *The Freedom of the City*, *Living Quarters*, *Aristocrats*, *Faith Healer* and *Translations*.

Dolan, Terence Patrick, *A Dictionary of Hiberno-English*, Dublin: Gill and Macmillan, 1998.

Etherton, Michael, *Contemporary Irish Dramatists*, London: Macmillan, 1989. An analysis of the major plays up to *The Communication Cord*, with an emphasis on structural elements. Includes an account of Field Day.

Flanagan, Deirdre and Laurence Flanagan, *Irish Place Names*, Dublin: Gill and Macmillan, 1994. A complete guide to Irish place-names, explaining the origin and derivation of the names of over 3,000 cities, towns, villages and physical features.

Hickey, Des, and Gus Smith, eds., *A Paler Shade of Green*, London: Leslie Frewin, 1972.

MacNeill, Maire, *The Festival of Lughnasa*.

Murray, Christopher, *Twentieth-Century Irish Drama, Mirror up to Nation*, Manchester: Manchester University Press, 1997. A comprehensive and valuable overview of Irish theatre from the Irish Dramatic Movement to the present day.

O'Brien, George, *Brian Friel*, Dublin: Gill and Macmillan, 1989. A concise, informative chronological introduction to Friel's work to 1989, with relevant biographical details. Useful chapters on his short stories, radio plays and his early stage-plays, with thematic links to his later writing. The plays from *Philadelphia, Here I Come!* to *Making History* are discussed in chronological and formal sections, with helpful criticism of his themes and approach, and a general overview of his place in Irish literary culture.

- *Brian Friel: A Reference Guide 1962–1992*, New York: G. K. Hall & Co., 1995. A chronological, annotated listing of biographical and critical information on Friel between 1962 and 1992; the guide cites books, articles, interviews and reviews.

Peacock, Alan, ed., *The Achievement of Brian Friel*, Gerrards Cross: Colin Smythe, 1993. A collection of essays covering various aspects of the work up to 1990, by scholars, theatre practitioners and historians including Seamus Deane, Joe Dowling, Seamus Heaney, Thomas Kilroy, Christopher Murray and Fintan O'Toole.

Pine, Richard, *Brian Friel and Ireland's Drama*, London: Routledge, 1990. A comprehensive reading of Friel's work to 1990 in the context of the development and significance of contemporary Irish drama and the development of modern Ireland. The book includes an evaluation of Field Day and contains a bibliography.

- *The Diviner: The Art of Brian Friel*, Dublin: University College Dublin Press, 1999. A revised edition covering the entire work up to 1997.

Roche, Anthony, ed., *Irish University Review, Special Issue – Brian Friel*, Volume 29 Number 1, Spring/Summer, Dublin: University College, 1999. This special issue brings together a number of distinguished contributors to honour the achievement of Brian Friel on the occasion of his seventieth birthday. They include Seamus Heaney, Frank McGuinness and Thomas Kilroy. There are also essays from several scholars, among them Anna McMullan, whose piece '"In touch with some otherness": Gender, Authority and the Body in *Dancing at Lughnasa*' is of particular interest here.